ASHE Higher Education Report: Volume 38, Number 2
Kelly Ward, Lisa E. Wolf-Wendel, Series Editors

Engaging Diversity in Undergraduate Classrooms: A Pedagogy for Developing Intercultural Competence

Amy Lee

Robert Poch

Marta Shaw

Rhiannon D. Williams

Discover this journal online at

WILEY ONLINE LIBRARY

wileyonlinelibrary.com

798294754

Engaging Diversity in Undergraduate Classrooms: A Pedagogy for Developing Intercultural Competence

Amy Lee, Robert Poch, Marta Shaw, and Rhiannon D. Williams
ASHE Higher Education Report: Volume 38, Number 2
Kelly Ward, Lisa E. Wolf-Wendel, Series Editors

Cover image by a_Taiga/©iStockphoto.

ISSN 1551-6970   electronic ISSN 1554-6306   ISBN 978-1-1184-5725-2

The **ASHE Higher Education Report** is part of the Jossey-Bass Higher and Adult Education Series and is published six times a year by Wiley Subscription Services, Inc., A Wiley Company, at Jossey-Bass, One Montgomery Street, Suite 1200, San Francisco, California 94104-4594.

For subscription information, see the Back Issue/Subscription Order Form in the back of this volume.

CALL FOR PROPOSALS: Prospective authors are strongly encouraged to contact Kelly Ward (kaward@wsu.edu) or Lisa Wolf-Wendel (lwolf@ku.edu). See "About the ASHE Higher Education Report Series" in the back of this volume.

Visit the Jossey-Bass Web site at **www.josseybass.com.**

Printed in the United States of America on acid-free recycled paper.

The **ASHE Higher Education Report** is indexed in CIJE: Current Index to Journals in Education (ERIC), Education Index/Abstracts (H.W. Wilson), ERIC Database (Education Resources Information Center), Higher Education Abstracts (Claremont Graduate University), IBR & IBZ: International Bibliographies of Periodical Literature (K.G. Saur), and Resources in Education (ERIC).

Advisory Board

Contents

Executive Summary   **vii**

Foreword   **xi**

Acknowledgments   **xv**

**The Need for Intercultural Competency Development
in Classrooms**   **1**

The Call for Intercultural Skills   2

Engaging Diversity for Intercultural Outcomes   4

The Promise and Challenge of Diverse Classrooms   8

Goals of the Monograph   9

Lessons of the Past   11

Tensions and Misconceptions   15

The Challenge of and Need for Integration   17

Student Voices: Reflections on Engaging Diversity in
Different Disciplines   18

Next Steps   19

Understanding Intercultural Competence and Its Development   **23**

Importance of Foundational Knowledge   23

Core Premises of Intercultural Competence   24

Building Blocks of Intercultural Competence   26

The Process of Intercultural Development   27

Outcomes of Intercultural Competence Development   39

Conclusion   43

Developing a Pedagogy That Supports Intercultural Competence   **45**

Institutional Context   46

Beyond Content and Content-Based Pedagogy   47

The Challenge of Intercultural Pedagogy   49

An Integrated Framework for Intercultural Learning   53

Intercultural Pedagogical Principles   55

Developing Intercultural Pedagogy—A Continuous Process
     That Happens Over Time   59

Classrooms as Privileged Spaces   60

Conclusion   63

Engaging Diversity Through Course Design and Preparation   **65**

Incorporating Intercultural Pedagogical Principles into Course Design   66

Conclusion   82

Practicing a Pedagogy That Engages Diversity   **83**

Applying Intercultural Pedagogical Principles to Classroom Facilitation   84

Conclusion   100

Summary: Conclusions and Recommendations   **103**

Notes   **107**

References   **109**

Name Index   **121**

Subject Index   **125**

About the Authors   **131**

Executive Summary

This monograph integrates multiple streams of literature that support the claim that the manner in which diversity is engaged in classrooms has a significant impact on the development of students' intercultural competence. The goal of the monograph is to synthesize literature on why intercultural skills matter, what they look like in practice, and how they can be developed by instructors regardless of the courses they teach.

The first chapter presents the social context that underscores the need for colleges and universities to prioritize intercultural outcomes. It establishes a contemporary understanding of diversity as a core institutional priority and resource, and proposes a framework of engaging diversity for intercultural competence development as one promising theoretical model. Diversity is seen as an essential thread that must be intentionally woven into the fabric of the institution at all levels, and defined broadly to include personal and social as well as visible and invisible forms of human difference. The authors argue that college classrooms are hopeful spaces where patterns of segregation can be interrupted and intercultural learning can occur as students experience cognitive disequilibrium and experiment with novel ideas. It is also noted that intercultural development is not a natural or inevitable process, and does not result merely from the presence of diverse social identity groups or course content. For the potential of diverse classrooms to be realized, instructors need a pedagogical framework for effectively engaging diversity to support intercultural outcomes. They need to know what intercultural competence looks like and what conditions foster inclusive engagement of diversity in higher education courses. Preparing graduates for the cognitive and intercultural complexity of the twenty-first century requires higher education practitioners to have an understanding of both *process*, what facilitates students' intercultural learning and development, and the *outcomes* of intercultural learning.

The second chapter provides an overview of key theories of intercultural competency development helpful to faculty who seek to design and implement classes that support both discipline-based and intercultural learning outcomes. This chapter presents research regarding the core skills, attitudes, and behaviors that are identified as requisite to effective and ethical intercultural interactions. Individuals with high levels of intercultural competence are inclined to respect others, seeing them as social equals. They display an attitude of openness, which presumes the acceptance of multiple ways of interpreting the world and withholding premature judgment. They are curious toward difference and tolerate the uncertainty and ambiguity inevitable in interactions with unpredictable others. The attitudes of respect, openness, and curiosity are foundational to the development of two kinds of knowledge essential for effective communication across cultural or social differences. One of those is cultural self-awareness, or an understanding of one's own culture and how it hard-wires basic assumptions, beliefs, and instinctive behaviors. The other kind of knowledge is sociolinguistic awareness, or the ability to give language meanings intended by the person we communicate with. Intercultural knowledge and attitudes work hand in hand with the behavioral skills and enable productive intercultural interactions. Those skills include listening and observing before evaluating, analyzing, interpreting, and relating to others. As a result of developing competence at each of three levels—affective, cognitive, and behavioral—individuals gain the ability to relativize their self in relation to others, and communicate with people different from them in ways that are both effective and appropriate. Interculturally competent individuals create new categories instead of relying on stereotypes and find ways to manage their own anxiety and uncertainty—skills that can be developed in most if not all college classrooms.

The third chapter provides the theory of how faculty can begin to think about engaging diversity for intercultural outcomes in their classrooms. Before one can implement specific instructional practices that support intercultural communication, one needs a pedagogical approach that reflects what is known on the nature of learning, particularly in regard to diversity. The authors propose a pedagogical model for faculty who seek to maximize the potential for a course to support students' development. They base it on Kolb's (1984) classic learning model, which imagines learning as a cycle of concrete experience, reflective observation, abstract conceptualization, and active experimentation. U.S. college classrooms rely heavily on cognitive content and do not provide students with sufficient opportunity to reflect and practice new knowledge. For college instruction to develop intercultural competency, it must follow three principles: maximizing purposeful interactions, valuing the assets brought by students to the classroom, and balancing dissonance with support. It is also noted that developing intercultural pedagogy takes time and requires the naming of the invisible forces of prejudice in the classroom.

The fourth and fifth chapters draw on the pedagogical framework developed in the third chapter, and apply the three pedagogical principles in the context of the classroom. In the fourth chapter, the authors identify evidence-based practices of instructional design that include building in classroom time for reflection and perspective-taking, structuring purposeful collaboration in diverse groups, incorporating opportunities to apply experiential knowledge, explicitly identifying desired intercultural skills as course outcomes, and establishing a supportive environment. These practices support students' ability to engage across disciplines in ways that are inclusive of multiple cultures and lived experiences and to value diversity in reaching common goals. The authors demonstrate how collaborative learning can be intentionally designed and implemented to facilitate interactions between classmates and with content whose experiences, identities, and points of view were different from each other. In the fifth chapter, the discussion shifts to the stage of implementation and focuses on the skills involved in facilitating interactions in a course that seeks to support students' intercultural competence. The authors highlight five pedagogical practices that support intercultural outcomes: acknowledging anxiety and offering support when dissonance threatens to undermine learning, disrupting social relations that involve segregation and bias, modeling the balance of suspending judgment and legitimate constructive critique, and facilitating conditions to support inclusive dialogue.

The authors conclude with a reflection on the historic meaning of "university" as a totality of a group unified for common benefit, and note the need for further research on engaging diversity for intercultural communication outcomes in all disciplines and fields. The authors note that faculty commitment to effective classroom practices must be matched with an institutional commitment for engaging diversity. Just as a classroom must align the environment, pedagogy, and instructional practice to engage diversity, institutions should also align institutional rhetoric with resource allocation, hiring practices, and curriculum in ways that move from espousing to enacting the value of diversity.

Foreword

Conversations about diversity abound on college campuses, ranging from encouraging members of the campus community to "get along" to engaging in dialogues about difference associated with power and privilege. For students to live in an increasingly multicultural world, developing intercultural competence is crucial to meaningful participation in society. Yet a recent study by Rude, Wolniak, and Pascarella reported in *Inside Higher Education* (April 10, 2012) provides alarming data. The study suggests that contrary to popular beliefs about the liberalizing effects of college as a time for students to learn about difference and getting along with others, for most students, being in college does not contribute to racial understanding, and for those students who do change, they actually become less committed to intergroup understanding. Such data suggest that faculty and administrators cannot rely on passive transmission of knowledge about diversity to create greater understanding of students. Classrooms can be one such place where faculty can move beyond a passive approach to developing intercultural understanding toward an approach that is deliberate and active—a stance that is likely to have more impact on students.

Engaging Diversity in Undergraduate Classrooms: A Pedagogy for Developing Intercultural Competence provides readers with very useful, timely, and empirically grounded information and ideas for how to actively engage in developing intercultural competence in students. Monograph authors Amy Lee, Robert Poch, Marta Shaw, and Rhiannon D. Williams take a very unique approach. They focus their attention on classrooms as pedagogical spaces to engage students in the development of intercultural awareness and competence. Too often, unfortunately, faculty are not aware of the importance of student intercultural awareness and competence, nor are they aware of how to facilitate and support this process in a meaningful and helpful manner. The purpose of this monograph is to provide faculty with tools they can use as they work with students in their classrooms. The monograph is very useful in that it provides readers with a rationale for developing intercultural competence in addition to the associated processes and outcomes. Relying on an integrated combination of existing research and practices, the monograph helps readers to understand the importance of furthering students' development of intercultural competence, a theoretical basis for doing so, how to create classroom spaces that foster students' intercultural competence, and how to develop campus spaces that support such work.

Recognizing that the creation of classrooms which develop students' intercultural awareness is not independent of institutional context, the authors also address the campus as a whole and its role in creating environments that foster student development with regard to diversity. It is important for institutions to not just call for commitments to diversity, as they often do, but to also back up the rhetoric by enacting agendas aligned with intercultural awareness and competence through changes in classroom practices for faculty and students. Lee, Poch, Shaw, and Williams do a remarkable job of not only pointing out the need for students to become interculturally aware, but more importantly they provide empirically grounded reasons for faculty to support students' intercultural development, as well as clear examples of how faculty can intentionally support this process. They approach the topic with different disciplines in mind, recognizing that it is important to develop intercultural competence for students in all areas ranging from the sciences to engineering as well as professional fields, social sciences, and the humanities. The authors are cognizant of discipline and different contexts in their discussion.

Engaging Diversity in Undergraduate Classrooms: A Pedagogy for Developing Intercultural Competence sits alongside other ASHE monographs that have grappled with similar topics. For example, Chun and Evans's *Bridging the Diversity Divide: Globalization and Reciprocal Empowerment in Higher Education* and Zúñiga, Nagna, Chesler, and Cytron-Walker's *Intergroup Dialogue in Higher Education: Meaningful Learning About Social Justice* collectively look at different aspects of creating and enacting diversity and conversations about diversity among faculty, administrators, and students. The monographs are not just "how to" manuals; they also grapple with the issues associated with and surrounding the importance of diversity.

Engaging Diversity in Undergraduate Classrooms is timely in that it provides an action plan to support the rhetoric associated with diversity that is commonplace on so many campuses. I gathered some great ideas from reading this monograph. As an administrator, the monograph provides me with tools to encourage faculty to recommit to diversity in their classrooms, why it's important, and to provide examples of what it looks like. As a faculty member, the monograph provides me with great ideas on things I can do as I plan my classes for the semester and different ideas for how to approach topics on a given day. I recommend this monograph to faculty wanting to change their classrooms, administrators wanting ideas on how to carry out diversity agendas, and researchers interested in related topics.

The monograph does a laudable job of addressing the micro- and macro-inequities that exist on campus and the role that developing intercultural competence plays in creating classroom and campus spaces that are deliberate in their approach. The monograph has the requisite combination of theory and practice to engage readers in deliberation about the importance of intercultural competence as well as the practical skills necessary to carry out such goals.

Kelly Ward
Series Editor

Acknowledgments

The authors would like to thank Kris Cory and Pat James for providing energizing, challenging feedback with lightning speed when we most needed it. We appreciate the research assistance and insights Kelly Winters provided during the early stages of this work, and the research assistance Chaltu Hassan contributed in the final stages.

Thanks to our students for being partners in engaged classrooms where diversity enriches our learning and lives. We are also lucky to have innovative, inquisitive colleagues who are exemplars of inclusive excellence in their teaching, research, and engagement.

Amy Lee is grateful to John Magers for his indefatigable support in many forms, and to A. J. Griffin and Timothy Lee for inspiration and timely laughs. Amy also thanks Annette Digre, Jennifer Franko, and Barry Stehlik, who helped make it possible for her to give adequate time to this project and offered unfailing encouragement.

Marta Shaw wishes to thank Kristina Tawse and Chad Rutter for their feedback and helpful suggestions on synthesizing the literature in ways that are helpful for instructors across the disciplines.

Robert Poch thanks Cindy Poch for reading and commenting on multiple chapter drafts and for patiently cohabitating with hundreds of books and articles on teaching in the narrow hall between kitchen and living room.

Rhiannon Williams thanks her coauthors for engaging in much debate, sharing of perspectives, and the exciting, yet sometimes draining process of writing on such an important topic.

Published online in Wiley Online Library
(wileyonlinelibrary.com) • DOI: 10.1002/aehe.20002

The Need for Intercultural Competency Development in Classrooms

Knowing that students and society could ultimately benefit from new approaches to cross-cultural learning, but failing to take the necessary steps to intentionally create enabling conditions [in and] outside the classroom is downright irresponsible.

[Harper and Antonio, 2008, p. 12]

EFFECTIVELY ENGAGING DIVERSITY is one of the highest priorities for higher education today, and we are not doing an adequate job. Current demographic, social, and economic contexts underscore the need for colleges and universities to comprehensively utilize diversity in ways that foster excellence and inclusion on behalf of students' intellectual and social development. In light of the pressing need to effectively support educational outcomes for an increasingly heterogeneous population, and to prepare graduates for the cognitive and intercultural complexity of the twenty-first century, higher education practitioners and scholars need a deeper understanding of how to effectively engage diversity.

The impetus for this monograph comes from our own experience, both in the classroom and in our research. In the past ten years, we have observed our institution's student population become increasingly diverse in terms of racial and ethnic demographics. Historically, generalized categories of racial and ethnic identity have become more diffuse and complex. We are also more mindful of the often less visible forms of difference that are present in any learning environment, such as socioeconomic status, sexual orientation, religion, disability, and many others. Among our students, there is a growing chasm when it comes to socioeconomic status, with an increase in representation of students from both ends of the income spectrum and thus the likelihood of significant disparity and diversity in both educational and lived experiences. For many students, whether they are from urban contexts or remote, rural areas, college is the first time they experience daily and direct encounters with individuals they define as "different." This isn't surprising given the segregation in U.S. neighborhoods and schools with regard to income, race, and culture (Saenz, 2010). Our students bring multiple dimensions of human difference and diverse social identities, and they also share some common aspirations: to graduate from college; to have choices about their career; to cultivate what they need to succeed; to provide for their parents and families; and to contribute positively to their neighborhoods and world. Many of them also express a commitment to addressing injustices and inequities in education and economic realities.

The students who attend our colleges and universities increasingly reflect the broad array of national and global diversity. They come to campus with different cultural backgrounds, languages, lived histories, geopolitical orientations, faiths, and educational experiences. When the four of us imagine our students after college, we know many of them will find themselves working together, living in proximity, impacted by common issues in the community, and sharing public spaces such as schools and parks. Yet when we look out at our classrooms, we often notice that students tend to segregate themselves physically, interacting with students who share visible identity characteristics. What students do not typically bring with them to college is a level of intercultural competence required to effectively interact across difference. Intercultural competence is broadly defined as the "ability to communicate effectively and appropriately in intercultural situations, to shift frames of reference appropriately and adapt behavior to cultural context" (Deardorff, 2006, p. 249). Considerable research has documented that students enter college with a lack of cultural awareness and understanding of what it takes to effectively engage diversity (Pascarella and Terenzini, 2005).

The Call for Intercultural Skills

In recent decades, intercultural competence has been increasingly recognized as a priority in educational outcomes of higher education. A significant amount of evidence highlights the benefits of diversity to student learning and development when that diversity is represented and actively valued and engaged. Studies identified cognitive, affective, and social outcomes associated with engaging diversity, in particular, increased cognitive sophistication and complexity (Antonio, 2004; Gurin, Dey, Hurtado, and Gurin 2002; Yershova, DeJeaghere, and Mestenhauser, 2000), critical thinking skills (Hu and Kuh, 2003; Milem, 2003), academic skill development (Denson and Chang, 2009), reducing prejudice, and increasing racial and cultural appreciation (Allport, 1954; Bowman, 2010b; Pettigrew and Tropp, 2006) and the development of leadership skills (Antonio, 2000). Repeated, deliberate engagement with diversity also contributes to the growth of higher-order cognitive skills, such as cooperative intergroup behavior, and openness to considering alternative views (Gottfredson and others, 2008; Hurtado, 2001; Saenz, Ngai, and Hurtado, 2007).

Policymakers and researchers have called for undergraduate education to systematically support the development of these skills and knowledge in order to enable graduates to successfully navigate a complex, diverse, and increasingly interconnected world (Association of American Colleges and Universities [AAC&U], 2007; Arkoudis and others, 2010; Deardorff, 2009a). A report published in 2007 by the AAC&U, "College Learning for a New Global Century," identifies intercultural learning as "one of the new basics in a contemporary liberal education," one that is "essential for work, civil society, and social life" (p. 15). Similarly, disciplinary associations across higher education in fields as diverse as engineering, business, medicine, agriculture, and education have noted the increasing need for attention to supporting the development of interculturally competent graduates (Grandin and Hedderich, 2009; Kumagai and Lypson, 2009; Moran, Youngdahl, and Moran, 2009; Sargent, Sedlak, and Martsolf, 2005).

Many employers have also called for higher education to better support graduates' development of the capacities to work productively and positively within professional environments of diverse cultures, views, and opinions (AAC&U, 2002, 2010; Dey and others, 2010). An employer-based rationale for diversity initiatives is important for faculty to note despite the frequent and warranted critiques that it focuses on the needs of already privileged populations who "need" diversity skill credentials, and thus does not support equity-related goals. It is important to question how various logics may produce programming that perpetuates differential benefits for student populations and ignore existing cultural capital that some students have developed. Yet in order to compel institutions to invest more resources and place strategic priority on the capacity to engage diversity effectively, a range of calls for change is necessary. This monograph proposes that a mindful approach is needed that foregrounds the objective of serving and benefiting all students.

The diverse voices calling for intercultural skills contrast sharply with evidence suggesting that, to date, students are still not being adequately prepared to participate and thrive in diverse workplaces and personal contexts. Findings of a recent national study based on the Personal and Social Responsibility Inventory (PSRI) led the authors to conclude that "while higher education places high value on engaging diverse perspectives, [institutions] need to do much more to ensure that . . . students actually develop these capacities across several years in college" (Dey and others, 2010, p. ix). Employers have likewise found intercultural skills to be in short supply among college graduates, highlighting their specific deficiencies in the areas of applying skills effectively in new contexts and adaptability to different cultural perspectives (Milem, 2003). There is also evidence of uneven results that tend to fall along disciplinary boundaries. Upon graduation, students majoring in business, science, nursing, and engineering report the least growth in relation to cultural competence (Pascarella and Terenzini, 2005). While organizations continue to look to higher education to provide individuals with the needed competence, the perception among employers remains that higher education is not adequately responding (Smith, 2010).

Engaging Diversity for Intercultural Outcomes

From Allport's (1954) classic contact theory to more recent studies on the relationship between intergroup contact and diversity-related learning and development outcomes (Denson and Chang, 2009; Gurin, Dey, Hurtado, and Gurin, 2002; Hu and Kuh, 2003), it is clear that both the frequency and quality of interactions with diversity are significant factors in realizing the benefits of learning in a diverse environment. In a meta-analysis of research on diversity experiences and cognitive development, Bowman (2010a) found that a diverse student body yielded educational benefits only to the extent that students had meaningful interactions with one another.

Across various fields of research, similar conclusions have emerged regarding the benefits associated with a diverse student population and multicultural course content. These benefits do not accrue passively or automatically (Alger and others, 2000; Denson and Chang, 2009; Gesche and Makeham, 2008; Marin, 2000; Otten, 2003). Rather, diversity must be actively engaged (Williams, Berger, and McClendon, 2005; Wong, 2006). These findings are important in that they suggest the importance of intentionally designed and actively facilitated intercultural interactions. Neither the institutional culture nor its participants and representatives (faculty, staff, administrators, students) are automatically willing or inherently competent to engage diversity effectively. It is also important to note that several studies have concluded that it is important to provide sustained and coordinated efforts across and throughout the undergraduate experience in order to maximize the benefits of diversity on student development and learning (Gottfredson and others, 2008; Gurin, Dey, Hurtado, and Gurin, 2002).

From engineers to educators, we all have an equal stake in and opportunity to support students' preparation for positive and effective participation in an increasingly interconnected, global society. While there is research to support the importance of the presence of structural diversity, it is inadequate to assume that its presence alone will result in an institutional culture that supports a robust exchange of ideas and perspectives (Alger and others, 2000). Simply enclosing a diverse group of people within the same four walls for four hours each week does not support students' development of diversity-related skills. It is not even sufficient to have diverse students discussing shared content and working on collaborative projects. While potentially valuable, these strategies do not in and of themselves compel substantive intergroup interaction or deepen students' competence and confidence in communicating in diverse contexts. What is needed is a "comprehensive model of transformational change that puts diversity at the center of the educational mission" (Krutky, 2008, p. 3)—a theoretically informed practice for designing and facilitating our classrooms in ways that engage diversity as an integral part of intellectual rigor and academic and professional excellence.

Foundational Assumptions

In this monograph, we integrate multiple streams of literature that support the claim that *how* diversity is engaged in classrooms has a profound impact on the development of students' intercultural competence. The concept of engaging diversity arises out of the theoretical framework of *inclusive excellence* (AAC&U, 2005) and is grounded in contemporary research on diversity and equity in higher education. The foundational premise of inclusive excellence is that educational quality and diversity need to be fundamentally and systematically integrated in institutional structures, curricula, and policies. This framework revises the traditional model wherein diversity is approached as a target or an outcome—as a "thing" that can be definitively achieved or counted, and that remains in the margins of institutional life. In an inclusive excellence framework, diversity is understood to be a complex and essential thread that must be intentionally woven into the fabric of the institution at all levels: policy, leadership, institutional culture, student life, and last but not least, the classroom (Clayton-Pedersen, O'Neill, and Musil, 2009; Milem, Chang, and Antonio, 2005; Williams, Berger, and McClendon, 2005). The fundamental structural revisioning described in this framework is demanding because it challenges the often deeply embedded and unacknowledged dominant discourses and practices in each of the institutional levels.

Accordingly, engaging diversity in the classroom is defined in this monograph as the "active, intentional, and ongoing engagement with differences—in people, in the curriculum, in the co-curriculum, and in communities in ways that increase one's awareness, content knowledge, cognitive sophistication, and empathic understanding of the complex ways individuals interact within systems and institutions" (Clayton-Pedersen, O'Neill, and Musil, 2009, p. 6). Engaging diversity in the classroom refers, therefore, to intentional, comprehensive efforts to develop and implement pedagogy that leverages the diversity resources of a campus for the benefit of students' learning and development.

There are two important components to note in our construction of the concept of engaging diversity. We define diversity broadly so as to be inclusive of the visible and invisible forms of human difference that impact identity development as well as interpersonal interactions (Harper and Quaye, 2009). This definition therefore includes individual differences (for example, personal history, life experience, educational background, learning style) as well as group or social differences (for example, race, ethnicity, religion, language spoken, socioeconomic class, sexual orientation, country of origin; Clayton-Pedersen, O'Neill, and Musil, 2009). Assuming this definition, all students are understood to bring diversity resources to the institution. While we tend to focus on the visible differences present in our classroom, there are always invisible differences that inform and can enrich or complicate the classroom experience for students and faculty alike. Recognizing and engaging all forms of difference may not be possible, but bringing multiple forms of difference into the center of the classroom space may facilitate awareness of how certain aspects of identity and lived experience are positioned by dominant discourses and their influence on concepts and beliefs about what is "normal" whether in relation to knowledge, communication, or interactions.

We are likewise mindful of the proliferation of uses of the term *engagement* and therefore of the importance of defining it within the scope of this monograph. In the literature on student engagement, the term refers to intent, capacity, and behaviors displayed by students, faculty, and other institutional actors. In reference to student behaviors, engagement refers to the amount and quality of time spent on educationally purposeful activities; in referring to the institution, engagement describes the resources and structures that facilitate students' participation in activities that support the desired outcomes (Harper and Quaye, 2009; Kuh and others, 2007). In using the term *engagement* in this monograph, we are signaling the importance of ensuring that the *presence* of difference in student demographics or course content is a starting point that subsequently facilitates the *act and process* of incorporating those differences in an intentional, purposeful manner. In other words, exposing students to diverse ideas, experiences, and perspectives is a necessary but not sufficient condition to foster the development of cognitive and affective diversity outcomes (Gottfredson and others, 2008; Gurin, Dey, Hurtado, and Gurin, 2002; Saenz, Ngai, and Hurtado, 2007; Umbach and Wawrzynski, 2005).

The Promise and Challenge of Diverse Classrooms

The classroom environment is an especially important space for diversity to thrive, and can potentially affect all dimensions of campus climate. Research has demonstrated the positive impact that a classroom engaged with diversity has on student outcomes, particularly when faculty, course content, and pedagogy are considered in conjunction with the compositional diversity of the students [Milem, Chang, and Antonio, 2005, p. 24].

Because students from varied backgrounds and social groups are drawn to common courses, the classroom is a unique space where patterns of segregation and poor communication found on the outside can be powerfully interrupted. Classrooms are natural environments where students gain knowledge about diversity, but they are also arenas of practice where students can develop, apply, reflect on, and refine the skills that are necessary for respectful and purposeful collaborations across difference. Classes in the early college years offer a particularly significant opportunity for cognitive growth relevant to diversity (Bowman, 2010b). As students enter college with established habits of mind and social interaction, experience with novel ideas, unfamiliar contexts, and diverse social groups can prompt the discontinuity or cognitive disequilibrium seen as critical to supporting cognitive and affective development (Hurtado, 2005; Milem, Chang, and Antonio, 2005). These are intercultural skills and behaviors that can be supported and developed across the curriculum. As noted earlier, we present the need to fully embed and integrate diversity across the curriculum as a mandate that fulfills the institutional mission to educate *all* students to its fullest capacity so as to prepare them to be effective citizens, community members, and employees.

As previously noted, however, engaging diversity in the classroom is not a natural or inevitable process, and does not result merely from the presence of diverse social identity groups or course content. In the same way that we cannot assume that intercultural competency skills will naturally develop as the result of a structurally diverse environment, it is problematic to assume that faculty have the awareness, skills, or knowledge necessary to engage diversity in their courses. In a multi-institutional survey conducted by Maruyama,

Mareno, Gudeman, and Marin (2000) of more than 500 faculty from Carnegie Research-1 institutions,[1] only one-third of faculty responded that they had adjusted their pedagogy as a result of increased structural diversity in their classrooms, for instance, by factoring diversity into the creation of student groups. Research and our own experience cause us to reject the notion that the poor record at engaging diversity stems from a fundamental resistance on the part of faculty to embed opportunities for intercultural interaction within their courses. Instead, we imagine an audience of faculty who, as Khaja and others (2011) suggest, are impeded by barriers of time, energy, and knowledge that translate into a lack of developed capacity for this work. In fact, research in higher education indicates that faculty report a willingness and openness to interculturalism and diversity in their courses, but also a struggle or lack of understanding regarding how to incorporate this into their teaching (Johnson and Inoue, 2003; Mayhew and Grunwald, 2006; Pope and Mueller, 2005; Rothwell, 2005; Schuerholz-Lehr, 2007).

Goals of the Monograph

The goal that guided the writing of this monograph was to apply existing research on diversity and intercultural competence to the question of how we as faculty can use the time we have in our classrooms and the resources our students bring to help support their ability to engage in a diverse society. The application of existing research leads us to contend that by intentionally engaging the diversity present in higher education classrooms, faculty across all disciplines can help students develop the intercultural competences that our students need to thrive as employees, citizens, and human beings in our increasingly interconnected world.

We contend that each classroom has the potential to foster the skill of problem solving in new contexts, the attitude of being open to multiple perspectives, or the practice of trying multiple approaches to tackle a complex question. This requires recognizing opportunities and creating an inclusive classroom climate that enacts the belief that there is intellectual value in a range of diverse perspectives and approaches to knowledge. Actively integrating diversity in courses across the curriculum is likely to pose different challenges, some of which will be specific to our field or disciplinary conventions regarding epistemology, pedagogy, and rigor. This may require instructors to unlearn "mindless" pedagogy, where mindlessness refers to "heavy reliance on familiar frames of reference, old routinized designs, or categories and customary ways of doing things" (Ting-Toomey, 2005, p. 226). Rendón (2005) describes how mindlessness—which she terms *agreements* and defines as assumptions and beliefs that we absorb and adopt uncritically through assimilation into our disciplines, fields, and academic contexts—can support the perpetuation of habits of mind and of teaching practices that do not facilitate multiple points of view, tolerance of ambiguity, or other cognitive and communication skills associated with both intercultural competence and equity pedagogy theories.

We have found that, to date, comparatively little has been written about the conditions that foster inclusive engagement of diversity in higher education classrooms, particularly in classrooms that do not explicitly serve a diversity requirement. Yet we believe that such a focus is important and necessary in professional development of faculty if intercultural competence is to be supported in our classrooms. This monograph attempts to bring insights of diverse branches of educational theory to bear on the practical question of how faculty can leverage the diversity students bring to class in ways that support their intercultural learning outcomes. We aim to demonstrate the breadth of research establishing a supportive relationship between the presence of diversity and various student development outcomes, and propose one way of approaching intentional design for such outcomes to be achieved.

This monograph assists faculty in identifying the opportunities available in our classrooms, reflecting on established norms that can inhibit or diminish our capacity to effectively engage diversity, and designing an intentional classroom environment that structures interactions between students in ways that value the existing diversity and enhance the learning outcomes. Presuming that frequent and longitudinal opportunities to engage diversity will support the development of the necessary levels of cognitive and affective development, it is important to provide these opportunities across the curriculum and over the course of students' undergraduate education. We contend that there is no classroom that cannot support the development of intercultural competence, no classroom so encumbered with disciplinary knowledge or content requirements that there is no opportunity for this work, no classroom whose educational goals will not be enhanced through deliberate, thoughtful, and well-designed integration of diversity into its pedagogy.

Lessons of the Past

John Dewey (1915) wrote that "there is all the difference in the world between having to say something, and having something to say" (p. 35). In the history of the treatment of diversity in U.S. higher education, many chapters have been tinged with what "we had to do" and not necessarily with a collective perception that we had something valuable to do.

Piecemeal Approach

Higher education institutions have long struggled with how to systemically transform campus climates so as to engage with and integrate diversity and develop intercultural competence (Harper and Hurtado, 2007; Kezar, Glenn, Lester, and Nakamoto, 2008). There has been a tendency to produce "islands of innovation" (AAC&U, 2005) where the cumulative effect is a piecemeal approach that targets diversity but does not embed it in a foundational way across institutional contexts (Danowitz and Tuitt, 2011; Krutky, 2008).

One example of this approach is incorporating a "diversity requirement." Certainly, diversity courses have value; the expanding research on these courses and our own experience teaching required diversity courses at three universities point to the complex and substantive potential of these classrooms to engage students in transformative intellectual work (Eisenchlas and Trevaskes, 2007; Hurtado, 2001; Mestenhauser, 1998). Nonetheless, the model of associating diversity-related goals or intercultural competency development with singular or isolated courses whose intent is to supply what some students are lacking or to provide a tangible affirmative space for students who have historically been underrepresented in institutional contexts suggests an early response to diversity that was informed by the goal of coping with diversity rather than embedding it in the fabric of the institution and at the heart of student learning. As one scholar suggests, at present, "the question is not whether or not we want diversity or whether we should accommodate diversity because diversity is clearly our present and our future . . . the real question is how do we build diversity *into the center* of higher education where it can serve as a powerful facilitator of institutional mission and societal purpose" (Smith, 2010, p. 3).

Need for Transformative, Integrated Approach

In spite of increasing conviction and evidence regarding the importance of developing intercultural competence, its "manifestations . . . in the higher education community, while sincerely conceived, are often unclearly rationalized" (Olson, Evans, and Shoenberg, 2007, p. vii) because it is not comprehensive or embedded across the curriculum. Past experience has shown that it is not adequate to assume that diversity-related learning and intercultural development outcomes will be "covered" in a required diversity course, an intercultural training, or workshops offered by multicultural affairs offices. As Chang, Chang, and Ledesma (2005) have argued, the benefits of diversity do not accrue by magic, and magical thinking "provides no guidance for campuses in assembling appropriate means to create environments conducive to the realization of the benefits of diversity or on employing methods necessary to facilitate the educational processes to achieve those benefits" (pp. 10–11).

Smith (2010) provides a useful comparison between higher education's ability to develop the institutional capacity to prioritize, embed, and interact with technology and its apparent inability to do the same in relation to diversity. It is commonplace that institutions have transformed practice, policy, and infrastructure in order to integrate technology. Once campuses identified technology as a strategic opportunity and a powerful resource to improve educational and institutional outcomes, they moved to create the needed infrastructure, capacity, and systems to engage and embed technology at every level of institutional life. Yet, as far as integrating diversity, Smith and others point out that institutions tend to opt for a "retrofit" approach. When institutions invest in the necessary infrastructure, including professional development, and comprehensive integration, the diffuse and positive impacts are quick to follow.

There is increasing evidence that institutions cannot continue to function well without integrating diversity through systemic transformation. The necessity to engage diversity is made paramount by projected demographics for college-age populations in the context of historical failure of primarily white institutions to effectively support diverse student populations; increasing research suggests that active learning and inclusive environments promote achievement for particular student populations. It is difficult to ignore the evidence that diversity is a strategic opportunity, a powerful resource, and a critical imperative for higher education and that it is necessary to transform how we conceptualize, value, and enact diversity.

Achieving an Integrated Approach: Writing Across the Curriculum as a Model

An example of a successful effort to overcome a piecemeal approach to the development of specific competencies in higher education comes from the field of composition studies. Much like intercultural competence development, composition scholars and practitioners faced increasing evidence that a single term of focused instruction was inadequate to produce desired writing competencies. It became clear that students were traversing a wide range of rhetorical contexts even at a single institution; what constituted effective research writing in a chemistry course did not hold true in a philosophy course. Definitions and associations even with the seemingly simple concept of "academic writing" vary widely across disciplines and even from instructor to instructor (Herrington and Curtis, 2000). There was an increasing understanding that context mattered, so rather than focus on assuming or teaching a universal set of norms or conventions for effective writing, teachers needed to support students' capacity to tune into the specific rhetorical context at play. In short, it became evident that no single course could teach students "good" writing. What emerged as a result were "Writing Across the Curriculum" models that sought to support students' writing development and competency through implementing longitudinal, integrated opportunities across the undergraduate experience and the adoption of writing-intensive curricula.

Developing intercultural competency, similar to developing competency in written communication, rests on knowledge acquisition in conjunction with building the capacity to implement that knowledge across diverse contexts; both of these competencies require *knowing about* and *knowing how to do*. Like good writing, intercultural competence cannot be transmitted through exposure in the form of content, lectures, or a single class (Mayhew and DeLuca Fernández, 2007). Developing students' intercultural competence requires a process approach wherein students are provided with regular opportunities across the curriculum to engage in intercultural interactions that are intellectually relevant to the course and purposeful to students' future capacity to live and work in diverse settings. Effective communication and collaboration across perspectives, life experiences, and identity also requires the ability to recognize and manage the anxiety and uncertainty that typically accompany communication or collaboration in new or unfamiliar contexts and with others whom we perceive as "different" (Gudykunst, 2005). These arguments speak in favor of incorporating intercultural development in higher education in a similar way as writing development—across the curriculum and across all disciplines.

Lessons on Faculty Development

One particularly significant feature of the Writing Across the Curriculum precedent is that its first principle stated that *faculty* needed training in order to build the capacity to *teach* and not only to *evaluate* writing if students were going to develop. This principle is transferrable to this monograph: it is essential to build faculty capacity to design and facilitate pedagogies that support of students' development of intercultural competence. Smith (2010) suggests that a lack of faculty capacity to support effective diversity interactions (our review of research suggests there is also a failure to recognize these opportunities) leads to unrealized potential for supporting diversity outcomes in our classrooms. Therefore, we define capacity as developing the resources and expertise, but also the recognition of the need and value to enact this through pedagogical practices.

Just as research indicates that intercultural competency skills do not "naturally" develop as the result of structurally diverse environment, faculty do not "naturally" develop the awareness, skills, or knowledge to effectively support students' capacity to engage diversity. This would exemplify the "magical thinking" rationale by Chang, Chang, and Ledesma (2005) referred to earlier. Instead, faculty need occasions of "cognitive disequilibrium" that facilitate developing awareness and skill to support diversity and diversity-related consciousness in their classrooms. This requires adopting a reflective and critical stance on entrenched concepts, such as what constitutes intellectual rigor, and practices, such as the privileging of "rationale" and objective knowing over situated and positional knowing. The following chapters of this monograph focus on building faculty capacity to engage diversity in the classroom by developing knowledge about the process of intercultural competence development, establishing a framework for pedagogy that engages diversity, and reflecting on practices of design and facilitation that provide an effective environment for engaging diversity.

Tensions and Misconceptions

Before moving forward, it must be noted that several tensions inhibit our capacity to effectively support intercultural competence in our classrooms. For instance, faculty often identify a tension between adequately covering core content and the pressure to incorporate new skills and outcomes into a course. Scholars have also noted the historical tendency to deposit so-called skills courses in the general education curriculum. This has the effect of preventing depth as students are not provided with a coherent or longitudinal opportunity to cultivate, refine, and apply the skills.

We discussed earlier the tendency for diversity-related initiatives on campus to be piecemeal or "add-ons" rather than structurally and comprehensively embedded in institutional mission, curriculum and pedagogy, and policies (Green and Shoenberg, 2006; Mestenhauser, 1998; Milem, Chang, and Antonio, 2005; Otten, 2003; Smith, 2010). This lack of a transformative approach can result in conflicts and tensions between identifying what is core or fundamental and what is supplemental or additional to course content and outcomes. Without a shift in how we perceive the core objectives of teaching and learning at the university level, we will continue to produce an either-or competition mind-set. This shift would be based on research that concludes that learning does not happen from mere contact but requires guided, purposeful opportunities for intercultural interaction, reflection, and refinement (Banks and McGee, 1995; Kumagai and Lypson, 2009; Ladson-Billings, 1995a; Olson, Evans, and Shoenberg, 2007). Faculty, students, and employers can encounter mixed messaging within institutional curricula when important skill-based intercultural development is emphasized or explicitly valued in some places within an institution and not in others.

There is extensive research on the conditions that support a culture of diversity in institutions and the role of institutional leadership providing the infrastructure to engage diversity as a resource. However, there is not a lot of clarity or guidance for faculty regarding how they can develop confidence and skills to structure their courses so as to intentionally engage diversity (Dey and others, 2010; Eisenchlas and Trevaskes, 2007; Gurin and Nagda, 2006). Most college environment studies focus on overall institutional environment or campus climate, not college classroom environment. Furthermore, the qualitative elements of interaction are less understood and represented in the research given a historical emphasis on employing quantitative-oriented research on diversity (Marin, 2000). In our extensive research for this monograph, we found it challenging to locate scholarship that focused on diversity or intercultural competence within the context of higher education *classrooms* and with the aim of directly supporting practice or teaching.

Some multicultural education scholars argue that there is not only a lack of available research, but also misinformation about existing scholarship, which may influence faculty perceptions about engaging diversity and developing intercultural skills. Geneva Gay (2002) observed that, while strong opinions about the importance or value of such education are held, "Many teachers are hard-pressed to have an informed conversation about leading multicultural education scholars and their major premises, principles, and proposals. What they think they know about the field is often based on superficial or distorted information" (Gay, 2002, p. 107).

Meanwhile, engaging diversity in college courses requires thinking carefully and mindfully about pedagogical approaches and resources that are culturally inclusive and view students as assets with valuable and diverse strengths and experiences (Ladson-Billings, 1995b; Rendón, 1994). It helps to create places of belonging where dialogue about human difference and diversity can occur (Williams, Berger, and McClendon, 2005). Pedagogical resources that engage diversity enable students to be empowered academically and faculty to be the facilitators of student intellectual and social development (Antonio,

2004; Marin, 2000; Smith, 2010). The specific instructional priorities we will develop in the latter half of this monograph focus on the intersections between inclusive excellence and intercultural competence.

The Challenge of and Need for Integration

Throughout this monograph, we have intentionally sought to draw from a diverse range of existing scholarship related to intercultural competence development, multicultural education, learning psychology, and culturally relevant pedagogy. Synthesizing core concepts and practices from such a range of theoretical frameworks is an inevitably risky endeavor. The effort to put them into dialogue so as to develop an integrative framework risks simplifying them and necessitates omitting substantive dimensions of each tradition. We recognize and caution the reader that each body of scholarship included in this monograph defines its central purpose in a different way, and each has historically valued particular methodologies and epistemologies over others. For instance, intercultural competence theory has focused on understanding and supporting the processes by which individuals develop capacity to effectively communicate across cultures, while multicultural education aims to support equity of access and attainment in educational systems by explicitly exposing and challenging racism and other forms of discrimination. Critical pedagogies provide powerful tools for deepening our understanding of traditional models of teaching and learning, problematizing the assumption that pedagogy or teaching can be neutral, and probing the ideologies and discourses that are embedded within and perpetuated by them.

Each tradition we draw on also poses significant critiques of the others. Critical race theory and critical pedagogy have critiqued multicultural education for being liberal rather than liberatory. Intercultural competence theory, however, has been critiqued by multicultural education scholars for not attending to the dynamics of power, oppression, and privilege that structure relations across cultural identity groups in and out of the classroom. Critical pedagogy is often critiqued for not being responsive to implementation at the level of individual or local sites of practice. In spite of the inevitable limitations and tensions inherent in integrating these diverse bodies of scholarship, we believe they provide complementary insight into the kinds of principles and classroom practices that can help us lead our students toward an enhanced ability to communicate and work with others who are not like them.

There is great potential in encouraging interplay across traditions of research that have concerned themselves with investigating diversity in educational settings from a range of focal points. This potential is evident in the recent increase in arguments for intentional synthesis from the increase in arguments for synthesis (Equality Challenge Unit, 2010, 2011; Hoffman, 2004; Krutky, 2008; Olson, Evans, and Shoenberg, 2007; Otten, 2003; Wong, 2006). In some ways, the theoretical dimension of our endeavor in the pages of this monograph resembles the hard but rewarding engagement with difference that we call for in college classrooms. Like the cultures represented by our students, the bodies of literature we draw on sometimes clash with each other in jarring and affective ways. Yet the occasional tension or disjuncture they produce is fully worth the richness of the pedagogical framework that is born out of the conversation. The inclusion of different research traditions enables a breadth of focus that spans both individual and social dynamics, both the visible and the unseen.

To extend the analogy further, just as the process of intercultural development begins with an increased awareness of one's own culture, we also find it essential to inform the reader of the disciplinary culture from which we depart. The cornerstone of this monograph rests squarely on the foundation of intercultural competence theory, which serves as the main framework for understanding the developmental process of the individual. Multicultural and critical voices enter the conversation to bring into focus the structural and systemic factors that condition interactions and shape classroom contexts, and to illuminate what classroom practices can support student competence at engaging with difference. As we will argue in the following chapters, pedagogy is a dynamic art that requires multiple concepts and theories as its inspiration.

Student Voices: Reflections on Engaging Diversity in Different Disciplines

Throughout much of this monograph, we present postsecondary students' voices on the experience of engaging diversity in the classroom. We do so in order to honor the belief, central to many of the theories included in this book, that in order to understand what is happening or can happen in the classroom, it is essential to listen and attend to multiple participants' perspectives. Students' reflections are invaluable tools for teachers who seek to engage diversity in the classroom and regular use of such formative feedback can help us attune more carefully to the complex dynamics of learning in our courses.

We do not offer student excerpts as "evidence" per se. Rather, our purpose is to include student voices and to illustrate a range of perspectives regarding the components of the learning environment that facilitated their ability to engage diversity on behalf of their learning, development, and communications. There is little qualitative documentation of college students' perspectives regarding the experience of engaging diversity in courses, particularly courses that are not explicitly about diversity or fulfilling a diversity requirement. We provide these excerpts to augment the extensive quantitative research documenting the impact of interactions in fostering intercultural awareness, knowledge, and behavioral competencies (Bowman, 2010a; Denson, 2009; Milem, 2003).

The student reflections used in later chapters were collected in first-year courses across a range of disciplines, as well as interdisciplinary courses. Lower-division college students have been described as a particularly important target population for engaging diversity because, while entering students come to college with established habits of mind and social interaction, providing them with direct experience with novel ideas, unfamiliar contexts, and diverse social groups can prompt the cognitive disequilibrium critical to supporting cognitive and affective development (Hurtado, 2001; Milem, Chang, and Antonio, 2005; Pettigrew, 2008). A majority of the courses in which the reflective learning journals were collected do not meet an institutional diversity requirement, and the faculty members who teach the courses represent a range of disciplinary affiliations range from biology to psychology to humanities, history, and mathematics education.

Next Steps

Although noble aspirations and expectations surround notions of diversity within higher education, it is not clear from much of the existing literature as to how faculty within the classroom can intentionally engage diversity to create excellence through inclusive student interactions and use of instructional resources (Dey and others, 2010; Gurin and Nagda, 2006). In this introductory chapter, we argued that engaging diversity for intercultural competence development is one promising theoretical model that conceptualizes diversity as a complex and essential thread that must be intentionally woven into the fabric of the institution at all levels. The remainder of the monograph expands on the foundational concept of "engaging diversity" by operationalizing it in the context of classroom—a critical site for implementing diversity-related goals.

The next chapter provides an overview on key theories of intercultural competence development for faculty who seek to design and implement classes that support both discipline-based and intercultural learning outcomes. Preparing graduates for the cognitive and intercultural complexity of the twenty-first century requires higher education practitioners to have an understanding of both *process*, or what facilitates students' intercultural learning and development, and the *outcomes* of intercultural learning. Without this knowledge, we cannot work mindfully across our instructional sites to support students' development over time. This chapter presents research regarding the core skills, attitudes, and behaviors that are identified as requisite to effective and ethical intercultural interactions and communications. It concludes with a focused discussion of the management of anxiety and its impact on supporting or precluding effective intercultural communication.

The third chapter develops a pedagogical framework for faculty who seek to maximize the potential for a course to support students' development of the capacity to effectively engage diversity. Before one can implement specific instructional practices that support intercultural communication, one needs a pedagogical framework that reflects what is known on the nature of learning, particularly in regard to diversity. Many graduate students and faculty do not receive extensive pedagogical training, and while many opt to attend teaching workshops, those do not always have the time to provide a depth of focus on the theoretical concepts rather than on the "best practices" or "innovations." The third chapter draws from pedagogical models that support intercultural and diversity-related learning to provide a synthesis of key attributes of a pedagogy that supports intercultural communication and collaboration.

The fourth and fifth chapters draw on the pedagogical framework developed in the third chapter, and move into classroom practice. They imagine the reality of a faculty member entering a classroom at the beginning of a semester and meeting a highly diverse group of students with vastly different life experiences, places of origin, primary languages, belief systems, economic backgrounds, and cultural identities. The fourth chapter focuses on the stage of course design and preparation, and the fifth chapter shifts to the stage of facilitation and implementation with students. Throughout these chapters on pedagogy practice that supports engaging diversity, we emphasize the importance of alignment between pedagogy components as well as of reflective practice. In the fourth and fifth chapters, we offer practical examples of classroom practice to demonstrate that development of intercultural competence can occur in any classroom when faculty are knowledgeable about and committed to intercultural outcomes. However, we acknowledge that it is easier to imagine and describe how to connect development of intercultural competence with disciplinary content when using examples from the humanities and social sciences as compared to physical sciences and engineering. As our own graduate training took place within the humanities and social sciences, we used those frames in developing many of the examples that follow in later chapters.

Understanding Intercultural Competence and Its Development

IN THE PREVIOUS CHAPTER, WE ESTABLISHED the critical need for college students in the twenty-first century to develop intercultural competence. We now turn our focus to what the literature says about intercultural competence and students. To be effective in guiding our students in their intercultural development, we must be mindful of what constitutes the building blocks of such competence and what is known about the process through which persons develop it. We have selected intercultural development theory as the foundation of our discussion in hopes that its broad appeal is considered relevant across disciplinary and ideological divides. Being able to communicate effectively across difference is as valuable for future engineers and doctors as for social scientists, and is considered a valuable skill by both conservatives and liberals, both those who are religious and those who are not, living both in the United States and abroad. The choice of intercultural competence theory as our main framework reflects a desire to practice what we preach and communicate effectively across the differences inevitably brought to this text by our readers.

Importance of Foundational Knowledge

King and Howard-Hamilton (2003) noticed that "achieving diversity goals is complicated by a lack of discussion regarding what attributes (knowledge, skills, attitudes) constitute cultural competency and little research on how competency develops" (p. 120). The analogy of writing across the curriculum used in the previous chapter illustrates the need for foundational knowledge in developing skills across the curriculum: in order for faculty across the disciplines to effectively support students' writing development, they need at least a basic familiarity with research on how writers develop and what components may facilitate or impede development. Without such basic familiarity, faculty may require and evaluate more writing, but it is not automatic that they will be supporting students' growth and development as writers. In the same way, this chapter aims to provide a basic level of familiarity with existing research on intercultural competence, particularly the process by which individuals develop it, and the key components and attributes associated with such development. Knowledge of foundational principles of intercultural development will enable faculty to make good use of the time and capacity of our classrooms, regardless of the discipline being taught.

It is with the classroom in mind that we seek to define intercultural competence, identify its key components, and describe how these components are developed. We also explore the barriers to developing intercultural competence that can emerge in the context of the classroom, and how such barriers can be reduced. The purpose of the chapter is to provide the knowledge to guide faculty's capacity to facilitate intercultural interactions in ways that maximize the potential for generating skillful communication with difference. Ultimately, this knowledge, when integrated with ideological awareness and attention to socially constructed norms that privilege some forms of human difference and subordinate or marginalize others, can facilitate instructors' and students' capacity to effectively and ethically engage diversity. Attention to this is infused throughout the discussion of intercultural competence, and is more fully explored in subsequent chapters. Our primary focus in this chapter is to review key research on intercultural competence in service of promoting pedagogical practices that can be used by all instructors across all disciplines to help shape a more peaceful and thriving society.

Core Premises of Intercultural Competence

Identifying and understanding the specific capacities required for effective and appropriate intercultural communication and the process by which individuals develop them has been the source of much creative research and vivid debate. Increased interest in the internationalization of higher education has influenced researchers to think more uniformly about the qualities of an interculturally competent individual. While theoretical frameworks and models differ in their purposes, scholars do achieve some useful commonality within their ideas of what it means to be interculturally competent.

First of all, scholars agree that an interculturally competent individual is aware that his or her interpretation of a situation is one of many, and is open to new information or alternative perspectives (Ting-Toomey, 2005). There is also broad consensus that intercultural competence is demonstrated through effective interaction with people of different backgrounds. Spitzberg and Changnon (2009) describe it as "the appropriate and effective management of interaction between people who, to some degree or another, represent different or divergent affective, cognitive, and behavioral orientations to the world" (p. 9). In essence, a competent intercultural communicator is one whose interactions with others are appropriate in light of the expectations of the other person's culture, and effective in arriving at shared meanings and desired outcomes (Cupach and Imahori, 1993; Spitzberg, 2003).

Interacting with others who think, feel, and behave differently from us requires a certain way of thinking, feeling, and behaving that is not necessarily automatic or natural, but rather it occurs as part of a developmental process (Deardorff and Hunter, 2006; Gudykunst, 1998, 2005; Pettigrew, 2008). Across the literature areas, scholars conclude that this process requires time and opportunities for refinement as they do not develop overnight or in a vacuum. In his seminal piece on cross-cultural learning, Adler (1972) asserts that it takes "a set of intensive and evocative situations in which the individual experiences himself and other people in a new way distinct from previous situations" for an individual to develop "new levels of consciousness and understanding" (p. 7). Consequently, current research in the fields of intercultural competence and intergroup dialogue emphasizes the need for a holistic approach that attends not only to the cognitive domain, but to the affective and behavioral domains as well (Batson, Lishner, Cook, and Sawyer, 2005; Bennett, 1993; Byram, 1997; Deardorff, 2006; Kegan, 1994; King and Baxter Magolda, 2005; Okayama, Furuto, and Edmondson, 2001; Pettigrew, 2008; Yershova, DeJeaghere, and Mestenhauser, 2000).

In the classroom context, while each instructor may target an area of knowledge, all of us play significant roles in developing the affective and behavioral development of our students through the way we structure and facilitate classroom interactions. While only select classes will teach knowledge about effective communication across difference, all classes where difference is present are sites, for better or worse, where students' attitudes and behaviors toward difference get shaped and solidified. A holistic understanding of intercultural competence as knowledge, attitude, skills, and behaviors that enable effective communication across difference elevates the significance of each classroom as a site of intercultural learning (Bennett, 1993; Kegan, 1994; King and Baxter Magolda, 2005).

There is also a degree of commonality among researchers that intercultural competence is not a static state that one can acquire or master, but rather a set of skills developed and displayed in the course of interaction and communication with diverse others. This view of intercultural competence emphasizes the importance of context, and the reality that contexts are fluid and shifting. Incorporating a critical theoretical lens, it is also important to acknowledge and attune to power differentials that are commonly associated with cultural differences and historical, lived experience. An individual does not learn to mindfully manage their anxiety, apply their understanding of privilege or attune their communication through course content alone; he or she gains these skills by having continuous and wide-ranging opportunities to practice and reflect. Because classrooms offer multiple opportunities to engage and practice communication skills in a facilitated environment, they are feasible sites for the shaping of intercultural communication competence.

Building Blocks of Intercultural Competence

The basic definition of intercultural competence is a good beginning point, but it provides little insight into its core components. Scholars in the field consistently identify three primary building blocks as part of intercultural competence (Gudykunst, 1993; Kim, 2005, 2009; Rathje, 2007; Pope and Reynolds, 1997; Spitzberg and Changnon, 2009; Spitzberg and Cupach, 1989). Spitzberg and Changnon (2009) observe that from the 1950s forward, the core components of ". . . *motivation* (affective, emotion), *knowledge* (cognitive), and *skills* (behavioral, actionable)" rose to such a prominent place in the scholarship that "to a large extent, all theories and models of intercultural competence rely extensively on these basic conceptual metaphors to guide their explorations. . . ." (p. 9).

For the sake of clarity and consistency, we have chosen to follow the terminology used by Deardorff, whose model of intercultural competence development we draw on extensively in this monograph. The component terms of her process-oriented model have the advantage of having been agreed on by 20 experts in the field, whom she asked to identify the knowledge and skills they felt were necessary for individuals to develop intercultural competence (Deardorff, 2004, 2006; Pusch, 2009). Deardorff's distillation of these expert-identified components within her model of intercultural competence development is broadly utilized within the literature (Pusch, 2009).

The Process of Intercultural Development

Deardorff's model of intercultural development suggests that an individual's attitudes lay the foundation for the attainment of knowledge, and ultimately the development of a set of intercultural skills (Figure 1).

In the developmental model, intercultural attitudes, knowledge, and skills pave the way for an individual to progress toward effective and appropriate behavior in intercultural situations. Intercultural development begins with the foundational attitudes of respect, openness, and curiosity. An intercultural mind-set is then developed through increasing awareness, knowledge of one's own culture, and the ability to tolerate ambiguity and create new categories (Bennett and Bennett, 2004; Deardorff, 2004; Langer, 1989). The strength of one's affective, cognitive, and skill development shapes the effectiveness of communication with others, thus impacting the behavioral domain (Deardorff, 2006; Pusch, 2009). Lasting changes in behavior toward others often result from a shift in the internal frame of reference toward a more relative view of the self. While not always essential for effective communication, such a shift "enhances the external (observable) outcome of intercultural competence" (Deardorff, 2006, p. 225).

FIGURE 1
The Process Model of Intercultural Development

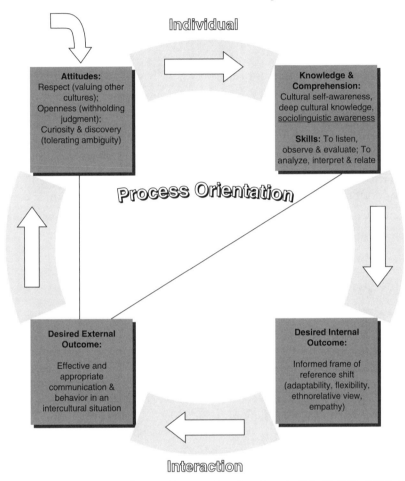

Source: Used with permission of Sage Publications, Inc., from Deardorff, D. K. (Ed.). (2009). *The Sage Handbook of Intercultural Competence* (p. 33). Thousand Oaks, Calif.: Sage; permission conveyed through Copyright Clearance Center, Inc.

Deardorff's model of intercultural competence demonstrates the cyclical, longitudinal nature of intercultural development. What is not quite clear from the diagram, but frequently emerges in the research literature is the reality of a dynamic interaction between the affective, cognitive and behavioral components (Deardorff and Hunter, 2006; Gesche and Makeham, 2008;

Otten, 2003; Pope and Reynolds, 1997). For example, affective qualities such as respect for other cultures and curiosity toward difference can motivate the acquisition of knowledge about other cultures, which can also assist in developing skills such as willingness to listen and relate to cultural positions that are different from our own. Interactions with other persons may spark a curiosity to seek out new knowledge about a particular event or group of people. However, focusing on the cognitive, knowledge domain of a student's development alone will do little to further his or her overall intercultural competence.

Component-based models such as this one are sometimes criticized for not clearly describing differences and relationships between components and stages of development (Spitzberg and Changnon, 2009; Van de Vijver and Leung, 2009). As Spitzberg and Changnon (2009) noted, these models have some theoretical weaknesses in that they have not sufficiently defined competence in relationship to "precise criteria" (p. 15); they also tend to attend to the individual more than the broader social context with its established patterns of power and privilege. Yet we would propose that the developmental model is particularly useful for educators in suggesting sequential areas of effort and action. Therefore, the components are worth examining briefly as they help to identify places where faculty can mindfully create opportunities for student development of intercultural competence while also exploring disciplinary content. The model holds the potential to inform what course design and content may prove useful in mindfully progressing among the respective components.

Domain: Attitudes

- *Respect* (valuing other cultures and individuals).
- *Openness* (withholding judgment).
- *Curiosity and discovery* (tolerating ambiguity).

Interaction with different ways of being and thinking about the world invariably elicits strong emotions. When we come into contact with difference, a natural response may be to flee from it or to resist it. Our attitudes about difference can either shut off possibilities for interaction or convert initially negative perception into useful questions about why we are reacting in particular ways, and what cultural meanings we may have missed (Bennett and Salonen, 2007).

Intercultural development literature leaves no doubt that attitude is a fundamental starting point for developing intercultural competence (Byram, 1997). Three elements in particular are viewed as "motivational," in that they cause persons to engage in a process that leads to further knowledge acquisition and skill development (Pusch, 2009). Scholars largely agree that three essential prerequisites to developing intercultural competence are the attitudes of respect for others and their cultures, openness to intercultural learning, and curiosity toward difference (Deardorff, 2004, 2006; Okayama, Furuto, and Edmondson, 2001). In order to support and identify them in the classroom, we look in more detail at how these attitudes are displayed, and what challenges we may face as instructors in attempting to foster them in the context of the classroom.

Respect.   Respect for others and valuing other cultures rest on a belief in their value and dignity. In intercultural relationships, respect is a deliberate inclination to recognize diverse others as social equals, manifested in a polite and empathetic use of language, including body language. Research using semantic analysis with participants from multiple cultures found that respect is broadly associated with polite communication, saving the face of another, and culturally appropriate eye contact (Arasaratnam and Doerfel, 2005). Lack of respect, however, is connected to behavioral symptoms of rude speech, not listening, and indifferent body language (Arasaratnam and Doerfel, 2005).

Although respect is a fundamental value in most cultures and educational contexts, college is often the first place when a generally respectful disposition becomes tested through close interaction with people with an entirely different frame of reference. It is frequently the case that diverse individuals present in the classroom differ in how they demonstrate respect. For many of our students, respect for others deepened in the course of hearing others' experiences and learning to recognize each other as equals. For some, such recognition necessitated embracing and owning their own voice. For others, it meant restraining their voice so that the voices of others were able to emerge and be heard. We share an example of an outspoken student who learned that respect for others is sometimes most appropriately expressed through silence. In her own words,

> My class experience has also taught me that sometimes it's better to keep quiet when everyone else is. I can be intimidating so when I constantly am voicing my opinion, not only does it get repetitive, but also I might be scaring someone else from voicing an opinion. The small groups have really helped me to work to do better with this. Rather than just voice whatever I'm thinking I try to reflect more deeply.

Respect figures prominently in institutional codes of ethics and student conduct policies, yet recent studies have shown that behaviors manifesting respect have been on the decline among college students in the United States. Longitudinal research has shown consistent and significant increases in narcissistic attitudes among college students (Twenge and others, 2008). Respect and valuing others are not attitudes that can be taken for granted on a twenty-first-century campus, yet they are essential for the roles that many students hope to assume in their society. Of course, respect is not something that can be mandated. One cannot stand in front of a classroom and demand that students respect diverse perspectives. As we will demonstrate in the fourth chapter, however, it is possible to design an environment that supports and models respect. An instructor may foster respect toward diverse others by providing time for students to interact with different perspectives and the contexts that influence those perspectives. One of our students reflected on the process of developing the capacity to respect diverse perspectives:

> I am a very opinionated person and when I feel like I'm right I don't like to be challenged. This class has shown me that it's not about being right or wrong, but it's understanding that everybody looks through a different lens. My interpretation and my classmate's interpretation may not be the same but that doesn't mean that one of us is wrong; it just means that due to different backgrounds and situations we may not look at the problem the same way. We . . . can describe this as our schemata. I've also realized that's a good

thing. If everyone were to think alike, we wouldn't be able to develop new ideas from the old ones. I've learned not to take disagreement personally rather than a learning experience.

Openness. Openness to intercultural learning and to people from other cultures presumes the acceptance of multiple ways of interpreting the world, and withholding premature judgment toward other worldviews, perspectives, and behaviors (Deardorff, 2006). In an academic environment, where critical engagement with ideas is valued and even required, it is essential to distinguish critical engagement from premature judgment. Openness is made manifest through behaviors such as active listening, attempting to see the world from the perspective of another, and clarifying assumptions and interpretations. It can be illustrated by the following reflection by a student on how small-group discussions and peer editing of student writing supported her development of openness, respect, and empathy for her peers:

> *The more [small-group editing and discussions] we do, the more comfortable we get with each other. One particular essay stands out to me because this individual revealed that they were gay. . . . Growing up in a strong Christian family, things like that are not really talked about unless it is concerning what the Bible says and what we know as sin. However, that was not my reaction to this hardly shocking news. I was happy that my classmate felt comfortable with sharing that news with me and the story that came along with it. . . . Now, going into a class where I am the only Christian or African American is not so much intimidating as empowering. I realize that I may be their only source of that particular group. This also gave me the opportunity to interact with other cultures or groups of people that I may have not communicated with, without this class. I feel more equipped to confront the other challenges that will be presented here at the university.*

This student reflection demonstrates that openness to others does not entail the loss of one's own identity or an embrace of unqualified relativism. Instead, intercultural competence involves a greater awareness of the factors that shaped one's own identity and a willingness to see the identities of others in their proper context (Ting-Toomey, 2005). Educational psychologists have found that many college students do experience a stage of increased relativism when a former expectation of right and wrong answers is replaced by a belief that all choices and perspectives are equally valid (Kegan, 1994; King and Baxter Magolda, 2005; Perry, 1999). The student above displays a more mature position of owning her beliefs while remaining open and empathetic toward the positions and perspectives of others.

Like respect, openness and empathy are critical attitudes that cannot be taken for granted on a college campus. Longitudinal research conducted by scientists at the University of Michigan demonstrated that college students' disposition to empathy has been declining since the 1980s, with an especially steep plunge in the past ten years. Since 2000, there has been a particularly troubling decline in the dispositions to consider the perspectives of others and to express empathic concern (Konrath, O'Brien, and Hsing, 2011).

Openness cannot be mandated, but can be fostered through an environment that supports and values the practice of openness to intercultural learning, which we discuss in more detail in the fourth chapter. A faculty member may support openness to intercultural learning by posing questions to students that elicit culturally or experientially informed responses to course concepts or readings, and by providing the time to engage the responses. A classroom that promotes openness to intercultural learning would, therefore, incorporate time for students to interact substantively with multiple perspectives within the course's content.

Curiosity and Discovery. Curiosity and discovery are attitudes that presume a tolerance for ambiguity and uncertainty (Deardorff, 2006; Pusch, 2009; Spitzberg and Changnon, 2009). Other cultures can be fascinating, but also scary in their unfamiliarity. To maintain a curious attitude toward other cultures and perspectives, one needs the ability to manage one's own anxiety in the face of that which cannot be predicted or explained (Gudykunst, 1998, 2005).

Ambiguity and uncertainty can be uncomfortable for students and faculty alike. In the context of the classroom, it can be difficult to promote tolerance of ambiguity due to the frequently unstated presumption that learning is a linear process in which knowledge is accumulated progressively and, in turn, diminishes existing uncertainty or ambiguity. Dominant cultural images of the professor in the United States tend to equate this role with certainty, absolute knowing, and mastery of knowledge. It is important for the faculty member to model curiosity and discovery if the goal is to support this attitude in students. For example, one might narrate his or her own learning history, perhaps including attention to deeply held beliefs or knowledge that came under question and were ultimately refined or cast away in light of interactions with new perspectives or knowledge. If listening is a key indication of openness, posing questions and pursuing the extension of new perspectives is a key indication of curiosity and discovery. Langer (1997) reminds us that this is part of the power of "conditional language"—language that does not communicate absolute answers but, rather, invites exploration and expression of alternative possibilities and perspectives.

Acknowledging ambiguity where it exists is also an important means of expressing this attitude. It might come in the form of making explicit that there are multiple legitimate ways to approach a problem, to approach a research project, or to interpret a historical document. A course that does not foster or model curiosity and discovery is likely to be one that emphasizes mastery of content, rather than application of relevant actions that can be taken by an expert in the field.

Knowledge, Comprehension, and Intercultural Skills

- Knowledge and Comprehension: Cultural self-awareness, deep cultural knowledge, sociolinguistic awareness.
- Intercultural Skills: To listen, observe and evaluate; to analyze, interpret and relate.

Research literature implies a close relationship between requisite attitudes and developing knowledge (Deardorff and Hunter, 2006). In Deardorff's intercultural competence model, the cognitive domain includes three essential components.

Cultural Knowledge and Self-Awareness. Cultural knowledge and self-awareness require the ability to explore one's own identity (ethnicity, language, race, religion, values, class, sexual orientation, and so on) in relation to the identities of others.

Cultural awareness is a central piece of the intercultural competence puzzle. In order to communicate well with diverse others, one needs a basis of knowledge about their cultures to put their words and behaviors in the appropriate context. For instance, in order to show and receive respect appropriately, one needs a base of knowledge about the culture of the person one interacts with. In the American context, it is perceived as disrespectful not to look someone in the eye. To come up with an accurate interpretation of the behavior of a Chinese student who does not look them in the eye, an American classmate or faculty member needs to be attuned to the different culture of the student. At the same time, they also need to be aware of their own culture and the associated hard-wiring of their instinctive reactions. It is only if they are aware of their own culture that they will be able to check the instant affective messages that are not always in keeping with cognitive awareness of a cultural difference—in this case, the affective message that the person who is not looking me in the eye does not respect me or has something to hide.

It is well documented in the research literature that interacting with cultural difference leads to greater awareness of one's own identity. By seeing who and what they are not, students discover who they are in ways they had never known of before. Knowledge of other cultures is essential for students to notice that they also represent a culture with an inherent set of values and assumptions.

In the context of a classroom, cultural awareness would be demonstrated through a student's ability to analyze and reflect upon their own lens and position in relation to peers' perspectives and the course subject matter. An individual who has a deep understanding of other cultures will also seek out multiple perspectives and opportunities to engage with difference in an effort to enhance his or her ability to critically think and solve complex problems.

An example of what demonstrating this competence may look like comes from a recent reflection of a first-year student, who articulates how course content provided the impetus for her and her classmates to explore their identities in new ways:

> *Then we talked about our cultures related to how we identified ourselves looking at what we are talking about in John's class. We*

talked about our family history and where we were born and how it affects us. Like Gloria talked about how she was born in Mexico, that geography had to do a lot with her identity of the people who lived in that area. For Najma, she mainly associated with her religion more than where she was from. She associates with Islam and it's part of her culture. For me, I identified with race not as much as place than either of them. It was interesting to hear about their different cultures. It was a very deep discussion of our identities that were outside of class.

By having students reflect on their own culture and participate in intercultural interactions, an instructor can foster a deeper understanding of cultural differences that leads to greater self-awareness. Without such intentional interactions, students will not automatically develop the ability to listen to their peers' experiences, reflect on their own identity, and directly connect the things they may be reading about to the people sitting next to them.

Sociolinguistic Awareness. Sociolinguistic awareness takes cultural knowledge into the realm of language. Like any behavior, language also reflects culture—even when it is a non-native language spoken in a foreign context. When Marta Shaw, one of the authors of this monograph, moved to the United States, her American accent led her professors to assume she was at home in U.S. American culture. Subsequently, when she responded to one professor's habitual greeting of "How are you" with truthful and lengthy answers, he found her off-putting and overbearing, while she perceived him as fake and unconcerned. If both sides had more sociolinguistic awareness, she would not have assumed that the question asked by the professor was anything more than a greeting, and the professor would have understood that in her cultural frame of reference, a question of this kind was not typically asked unless the speaker actually wanted to hear the answer.

In the research literature, sociolinguistic awareness (sometimes referred to as sociolinguistic competence) has been defined as the ability to give language "the meanings which are taken for granted by the interlocutor or which are negotiated and made explicit with the interlocutor" (Byram, 1997, p. 48).

The need for such ability will be readily recognized by any instructor who has ever taught a student from another country who always says "no" when asked if he or she understands, or never says "please," or always agrees with the instructor in class. Sociolinguistic awareness is what allows students and faculty to better interpret the verbal behaviors of others by recognizing how their language choices are determined by the context, the relationship between those communicating, and the cultures they represent (Arasaratnam and Doerfel, 2005; Van Ek, 1986). Effective communication across difference requires that we "try to understand strangers' meanings and try to make sure that they understand our meanings" (Gudykunst, 2005, p. 290). Interpreting others' language choices requires a knowledge of their cultures that is beyond the scope of any single college course. What each class can model and develop, however, are the habits of actively listening and suspending judgment, assuming that the other person acted rationally in choosing particular words or actions, and attempting to see what their reasons might be.

Further, all instructors can and should guide their students into the social and linguistic norms of their disciplines. Since graduates of colleges and universities are increasingly required to cross disciplinary boundaries in their professional work, they need the knowledge and skills that will enable them to communicate effectively with members of not just other cultures but also other disciplines. Academic and professional fields often form cultures of their own, many of them far from obvious to students. For example, discipline-based traditions of discourse are manifest in expectations related to writing in all fields, although these sociolinguistic norms are not always acknowledged by the instructor. Gallagher and Lee (2008) offer an example of the challenges faced by a certain student who graduated from STEM-focused preparatory high school (science, technology, engineering, math) and then took a college-level literature course. He was confounded by the writing assignments, including not only stylistic norms of voice and style, but also norms related to evidence and substantiating findings. While the elements of evidence, analysis, and findings are common to scientific and literary analysis, the norms that govern writing in these two disciplines are distinct. His writing reflected a particular training in the STEM disciplines: short paragraphs; statements of perceived results and findings rather than of interpretation; emphasis on reporting fact; and a detached authorial stance. It was necessary for this student to bring his existing skills to bear on a new form and product of inquiry. The development of disciplinary awareness fosters skills similar to those required for intercultural competence. In each discipline, we learn a new kind of language and interactive norms, and as we move across disciplinary boundaries, we grow in our capacity to adapt to differing intellectual forms. Traversing disciplinary discourse norms parallels in some ways the development of skills to interact effectively within multiple kinds of human difference.

Intercultural Skills. Intercultural skills are not simply learned from a text-book or from exposure to the right content; they are also not just a matter of positive attitudes toward diversity (Deardorff, 2004; Pope and Reynolds, 1997; Trimble, Pedersen, and Rodela, 2009). As research in multicultural education has long acknowledged, knowledge about diverse cultures and a favorable disposition toward them are not the same as the ability to respectfully and reciprocally engage difference, or to effectively interact and communicate within diverse settings (Bennett and Salonen, 2007; Krutky, 2008; Paige, 1993). Interaction between persons—not content or teaching materials alone—must occur for students to practice and develop intercultural skills.

The emphasis within the intercultural skills component is on behavioral ability to engage in intercultural interactions in ways that are informed, interpretive, and capable of producing positive relational results. In developing skills, time and space are needed to try and practice something that is not completely familiar or utilized regularly. This applies to what on the surface may seem very familiar, such as *listening, observing, and evaluating* (Deardorff, 2004). These acts occur daily, but perhaps are not practiced or used in ways that facilitate effective intercultural communication. For example, students in classrooms routinely listen to content, observe instructors and peers, and evaluate new ideas; they may also prove able to recount what the topic of the day was and main points made. Yet, without deliberate guidance, they often form immediate and fixed opinions, and are challenged in considering alternative possibilities. Ting-Toomey and Kurogi (1998) describe the skills required for intercultural communication as "mindful listening," "mindful observation," and "collaborative dialogue." A person who is competent in these intercultural skills would be capable of recognizing that there can be value in actively listening to an alternative perspective and being accountable to represent it accurately without first interjecting a dissonant point of view.

Regardless of the discipline they teach, college instructors play a crucial role in teaching and modeling how to *analyze, interpret, and relate* to others before forming judgments. For example, inviting students to explore diverse disciplinary or experiential lenses pertaining to a common concept can support this process by providing an opportunity to explore multiple frames of reference and come to their own interpretation related to both their own experiences and ones presented in class.

A specific example of this comes from a social science class session in which the term *American* was a core concept of study. *American* is a complex term, subject to interpretation and informed by experience and vantage point, but it is frequently assumed to have a literal referential meaning. In the class session, students discussed course readings that presented multiple disciplinary and cultural lenses on this concept. The discussion invited them to contribute analysis that connected their lived experience to the readings. This activity invited students to analyze various perspectives, including those of their peers, and to consider the interplay among them, making explicit how a particular concept, "Americanness," is highly contested and necessarily subject to interpretation. In creating a classroom environment where different interpretations of the term *American* were invited, presented, and discussed, the instructor enabled students to experience the value of suspending—or even confronting—judgments about word meanings until peer interpretations and referential meanings were heard. In the process, some interpretations of the term shifted and the value of listening and communicating across difference advanced.

Outcomes of Intercultural Competence Development

According to Deardorff (2004) and others, developing the attitudes, knowledge, and skills described in previous sections builds desirable internal and external learning outcomes. First, intercultural development often leads to a shift in the internal frame of reference, or "relativizing one's self" (Byram,

1997, p. 34). Such a shift in the frame of reference is not always essential for effective intercultural communication, but it is a stage of development that transcends the ethnocentric and narcissistic positions that have been spreading on college campuses in recent years (Konrath, O'Brien, and Hsing, 2011).

Second, intercultural development along the lines described earlier produces an increased competence at effective and appropriate communication across difference. The remainder of this chapter integrates Deardorff's model with other strands of intercultural competence research to address what such competence looks like in practice in order to set the stage for what this research implies for a well-informed design of college classrooms. What, then, does effective intercultural communication look like in the classroom?

Creating New Categories

The first significant characteristic of effective intercultural communicators is that they create new categories for diverse strangers instead of relying on old paradigms and cultural stereotypes (Gudykunst, 1998, 2005; Langer, 1997; Stephan and Stephan, 1985). When an individual is mindfully open to new information, he or she is less likely to mindlessly rely on "familiar frames of reference, old routinized designs, or categories and customary ways of doing things" (Ting-Toomey, 2005, p. 226). On the foundations of openness, cultural knowledge, and intercultural skills, individuals can develop the mental habit of contextualizing information and adjusting their ways of thinking to progressively emerging knowledge. The ability to create new categories is all the more valuable because it is essential for intellectual and social development in general (Langer, 1997). Since both require openness to new intellectual and social possibilities, engaging students in important disciplinary content can go hand in hand with develop and deepen their intercultural competence, as both require openness to new intellectual and social possibilities and communication.

Managing Anxiety and Uncertainty

Because intercultural interaction is always accompanied by some level of uncertainty, its effectiveness depends on the degree to which individuals can manage their own anxiety in relating to the intercultural other (Gudykunst, 1993,

1998, 2005). Stephan and Stephan (1985) explain that anxiety has to do with the fear of negative consequences for the self and negative evaluation by members of other groups. Anxiety is what prevents students from interacting on their own volition with others they perceive as belonging to a different group.

Managing anxiety and uncertainty has been studied in greatest detail by Gudykunst (1993, 1998, 2005), who reaches some surprising conclusions about the role of these abilities in intercultural communication. He concludes in his research that effective intercultural communication requires very similar knowledge and skills as communication between strangers from similar groups. Therefore, each individual has some cognitive and behavioral resources to communicate across diversity. The difference, according to Gudykunst (2005), lies in the levels of uncertainty and anxiety brought to the interaction. Therefore, even though we have much of the knowledge and skills required to communicate across difference, our own anxiety gets in the way when the uncertainty exceeds the level of our comfort.

Gudykunst (2005) notes that "what constitutes uncertainty depends on what we want to be able to predict, what we can predict, and what we might be able to do about it" (p. 16). Our classrooms at the beginning of each semester are a site of much uncertainty, as the majority of our students are strangers to one another. When they initiate interactions, they usually begin with someone they perceive as belonging to their "ingroup"—someone about whom they believe they can predict enough information to feel safe. Yet no one person shares all group memberships with another, so "everyone we meet is a potential stranger" (Gudykunst, 2005, p. 285). The difference between students interacting with students from their perceived "ingroup" and "outgroup" is not necessarily the skills that they bring to the communication but the ability of individuals to make predictions and manage their anxiety about that which cannot be predicted. While life is by nature unpredictable, interacting within one's group gives one a sense of security. "Uncertainty is a cognitive phenomenon; it affects the way we think about strangers" (p. 286). When individuals can see that there is a potential reward for them, or that they will meet the stranger again, they are more likely to try to manage their uncertainty. If we feel that interacting with strangers is not commensurable with the potential rewards, we are much less likely to make an effort to manage our uncertainty.

It is evident in the research literature that effective intercultural communicators are those who have developed strategies to manage their emotions and instinctive reactions toward those who are different from them. This is in contrast to the frequent assumption that effective intercultural communicators are those who do not "notice" or "mind" difference and who are likely to deny or suppress the presence of anxiety or uncertainty in intercultural interactions. Gudykunst's research does not suggest that the goal is to eliminate uncertainty, but rather to recognize and manage it in interactions.

Other Pieces of the Intercultural Puzzle

Intercultural competence theory offers foundational explanations of how and why individuals develop the capacity to relate across difference. As such, it provides an important part of the puzzle for those who seek to facilitate this capacity in students. What it does not account for, however, is the broader social context of intercultural communication, in which participants hold different amounts of power and play different social roles. Given the historical and socioeconomic differentials between our students, we must also recognize the fundamentally political nature of interactions that involve taken-for-granted norms and relations between different groups of people.

The components of the process model reviewed in this chapter beg many of the questions explored in scholarship on critical pedagogy. For example, the affective commitment to respect, openness, and curiosity found in intercultural competence development scholarship often demands that we consider ideas and perspectives that differ ideologically from those that we developed through previous experience or education. Capacities to value other cultures, withhold judgment, and develop cultural self-awareness are helpful in developing the kind of ideological awareness advocated by critical pedagogy. As we develop them, we begin to critically examine norms of thinking dominant in our culture or social class that we may have previously accepted without conscious thought. While explicit connections between intercultural competence theory and critical pedagogy are addressed later in the book, it is worth noting here that these domains of scholarship complement one another in a shared commitment to interrupt cultural and personal patterns that inhibit respectful interaction with alternative views. Developing intercultural competence increases awareness of one's own culture and the value of alternative perspectives (Bennett and Bennett, 2004; Deardorff, 2004; Langer, 1989). A possible result is a foundational shift in our internal frames of reference that create greater openness to intellectual and social possibilities that differ from the historically dominant positions of our particular culture.

Conclusion

In its simplest expression, intercultural competence development is about the capacity of individuals to respectfully engage and communicate with another so that they have benefit of another person's cultural perspectives. Such capacity results in the ability to communicate and form relationships more effectively with persons who are different from us, and to see, interpret, understand, appreciate, and utilize what we have learned in new ways. The development and the demonstration of intercultural competence come in the diverse and authentic sites of practice. Effective behavioral change requires rigorous cognitive development in addition to opportunities to apply and refine theory in integration with practice (Mayhew and DeLuca Fernández, 2007). Therefore, faculty can support the holistic process of intercultural competence development through well-informed pedagogy, including design and practice.

As Deardorff (2009b) notes, "in the end, intercultural competence is about our relationships with each other and, ultimately, our very survival as the human race, as we work together to address the global challenges that confront us" (p. 269). The weight of intercultural communication for the future of our societies demands that our classrooms provide the space and opportunity for students to engage each other, even when it is difficult and anxiety producing to do so. In the next chapter, we propose a framework for pedagogy to inform how faculty may structure and facilitate opportunities to engage diversity in the classroom in ways that acknowledge and work to support benefits for students of all backgrounds and cultures.

Developing a Pedagogy That Supports Intercultural Competence

Education in the twenty-first century must prepare students for a world that is increasingly interconnected, interdependent, and diverse. It is often difficult in such a world to communicate effectively, to form and maintain relationships and work cooperatively with people of different backgrounds. The need for these enhanced interpersonal skills across cultures is also evident domestically as U.S. society becomes more diverse.

[Krutky, 2008, p. 3]

AS WE ESTABLISHED IN THE PREVIOUS CHAPTER, intercultural competence development "is not a static requirement to be checked off a list but . . . the continuous critical refinement and fostering of a type of thinking and knowing" (Kumagai and Lypson, 2009, p. 783). It is clear that no single course or experience can fully "teach" students how to effectively communicate, relate, and work cooperatively with people of different backgrounds. To gain the necessary intercultural skills, students need ongoing practice and multiple opportunities to grow, staged over time and in new and changing contexts.

In the remaining chapters, we review research on pedagogy and recommend a pedagogical approach that supports the longitudinal process of intercultural development by engaging diversity across the curriculum. Incorporating key concepts developed in prior chapters, we shift the focus to the classroom in order to identify pedagogical components that foster engagement with diversity and intercultural competence development. The purpose of this chapter is to provide a synthesis of theory from current research on learning, multicultural education, and intercultural competence theory in order to articulate core principles that can guide effective intercultural pedagogy. To place those in the appropriate context, we also explore systemic factors that affect what instructors can realistically set out to accomplish when faced by the competing pressures inherent in today's academic workplace. The fourth and fifth chapters focus on two specific dimensions of intercultural pedagogy, designing and facilitating classroom environments, and elaborate on practices that facilitate effectively engage diversity.

Intercultural competence and the pedagogical capacity to support it are similar in that both are processes that develop in the course of time, practice, and reflection. The capacity for faculty to engage diversity in the classroom relies on a nexus of factors including intention, awareness, knowledge, and skills developed over time. Therefore, we concur with Krutky's (2008) assertion that, "Education in the twenty-first century must prepare students for a world that is increasingly interconnected, interdependent, and diverse" (p. 3). However, we would further assert that it is critical to *teach teachers* how to support these outcomes through substantiated learning about pedagogy and instructional design.

Institutional Context

The presumed reality is that most of us encounter heterogeneous groups of students who bring with them diverse of ways of being, knowing, and communicating. As established in the first two chapters, the mere presence of such diversity in the classroom does not ensure that students will automatically learn to communicate across difference. Even on campuses that explicitly promote diversity or internationalization initiatives, social environments and academic assignments tend to remain "monocultural, monolingual, and monodisciplinary" (Otten, 2003, p. 14). Many researchers have concluded that the impact of interactions may be as significant as the formal curriculum for longitudinal learning outcomes; enhanced intercultural learning and development depend in large part on how the interactions between diverse students are structured both inside and outside the classroom. Engaging diversity in the classroom begins with an honest examination of what instructors face when they attempt to support intercultural learning outcomes.

As we noted earlier, studies indicate that faculty are willing and open to teaching in ways that support intercultural competence, but a lack of knowledge about how to do it, combined with a lack of time to learn, leads to a disconnect between intention and outcome (Johnson and Inoue, 2003; Otten, 2003). In some settings, student resistance is also a significant factor—for instance, a study of faculty multicultural attitudes and challenges at one Midwestern university found student resistance to multicultural teaching to be the top concern of faculty (Khaja and others, 2011). In the past, multicultural teaching focused on diversity courses and co-curricular activities to increase students' sensitivity (Chávez, 2011), an approach that played an important role but also generated a good deal of resistance by enabling an "'us' versus 'them' mentality" (Khaja and others, 2011, p. 22). In light of these concerns cited by faculty, as well as the realities of inadequate resources, time constraints, and a lack of knowledge about multicultural pedagogy (Khaja and others, 2011), we accept that resistance to past methods of engaging diversity must be considered a part of the educational landscape that we occupy as college instructors. Given that the perception of such resistance tends to deter intercultural learning, we postulate the need to shift from a content-focused pedagogical paradigm to a way of learning that utilizes diverse viewpoints in productive and rewarding ways across the curriculum.

Beyond Content and Content-Based Pedagogy

Historically, there has been a predominant approach to engaging diversity through content, and as an "add-on" to existing pedagogy and curriculum (McGee Banks, and Banks, 1995; Dobbert, 1998; Green and Shoenberg, 2006; Mestenhauser, 1998; Smith, 2010). While this has yielded a general increase in the inclusion of diverse content and perspectives across a range of courses, it has also left unchallenged the assumption that the "real" or fundamental core of a given course is disconnected from the process through which it is acquired (Green and Schoenberg, 2006; Smith, 2010). The focus on content also perpetuates the misconception that some disciplines, such as the humanities and arts, are readily multicultural, while others, like the physical and biological sciences, are not (Banks, 1993; Mestenhauser, 1998).

Multicultural education theory has identified and focused on five essential dimensions: content integration, pedagogy, environmental or institutional culture, prejudice reduction, and knowledge construction. While Banks (1993) acknowledges that some dimensions will be more readily accessible or self-evident to faculty in particular disciplines, he also emphasizes the importance of an integrated approach that activates multiple dimensions. Scholarship on internationalization of the curriculum has grown in the recognition that international content additions to courses have done nothing to shift the dominant knowledge-driven paradigm for teaching and learning (Van Gyn, Schuerholz-Lehr, Caws, and Preece, 2009). There is also increasing visibility of efforts to construct a multifaceted and inclusive model of intercultural competence development that looks at the intersections with critical and transformational learning pedagogies (Eisenchlas and Trevaskes, 2007; Hanson, 2010; Van Gyn, Schuerholz-Lehr, Caws, and Preece, 2009). Across these strands of relevant research, one can find either an emerging or a sustained recognition that it is impossible to support intercultural communication and collaboration without acknowledging the reality that social and cultural identities have not held equal status or coexisted in an easy pluralism, in classrooms or elsewhere. Power, "voice" (as defined by both feminist and critical race theory), and privilege have been demonstrated to self-perpetuate in relation to social identities.

Critical pedagogy, multicultural, and intercultural education scholars also agree that the entrenched persistence of the content-focused model of pedagogy in higher education is problematic. Effectively supporting intercultural competence across the undergraduate experience requires challenging the traditional model that prioritizes knowledge acquisition as the critical foundation of undergraduate learning (Bennett and Salonen, 2007; Krutky, 2008). Rigor in academic contexts across a majority of traditional disciplines has been associated primarily with the cognitive domain, which has in turn perpetuated an expert-centered pedagogy that emphasizes traditional approaches (Mayhew and DeLuca Fernández, 2007). According to Langer (1997), the belief in the primacy of an uncritical absorption of disciplinary knowledge actually supports outcomes contradictory to its intention. Langer and Moldoveanu (2000) explained that "when we learn the basics mindlessly so that we no longer have to think about them, we are not in the position to vary them readily as we get more information about the task" (p. 3). In other words, the content model does not directly cultivate the capacity to adapt information to changing contexts, to problem solve, or to apply knowledge in diverse situations.

Content-focused pedagogy may have the advantage of allowing for more material to be conveyed, but this approach leaves little time for faculty to facilitate interaction with the material or its mindful application. In a content-focused classroom, students may become more aware of multiple perspectives, disciplinary lenses, or cultural discourses; but they are not likely to develop the skills and understanding necessary to actually apply this awareness in specific contexts. There is, an increasing amount of evidence and a growing recognition that interactive learning environments are actually more rigorous, since "traditional didactic classrooms (lecture, presentation, research projects) are effective for transfer of knowledge but not development of affective and behavior goals such as reflective application of new knowledge" (Mayhew and DeLuca Fernández, 2007, p. 57).

Engaging diversity effectively requires a focus on how and not only what we teach (Danowitz and Tuitt, 2011). This requires a basic but fundamental shift in how we conceptualize instruction so that it is designed and implemented based on a recognition that the acts of knowing and communicating are as dynamic and complex as we increasingly understand the world to be. Therefore, engaging diversity necessitates asking and acting upon different kinds of questions about our teaching so that our pedagogies are led not only by our content knowledge as accumulated through intensive disciplinary training and practice but also by intensive consideration on how to generate inclusive classroom conversation around ideas and concepts that are authentically open to individual and group interpretations and additions. It is an ongoing process — it involves acts of forming and re-forming classroom interactions that deliberately bring students into substantive and highly interactive conversation between themselves and our subjects.

The Challenge of Intercultural Pedagogy

"Pedagogy" is a more complex and extensive term than "teaching," referring to the integration in practice of particular curriculum content and

design, classroom strategies and techniques, a time and space for the practice of those strategies and techniques, and evaluation of purposes and methods [Simon, 1988, p. 371].

Pedagogy identifies the connections between the who, the what, and the how of teaching and learning. If we do not acquire the concepts or practices at some level of formal training related to pedagogy (whether by studying research on learning, or through reflective practice on our teaching or student experience), we are less capable of making intentional, informed decisions about how we organize, design, and implement our courses in particular ways. We are also less capable of recognizing and responding to whether and for whom the way we are teaching is indeed achieving our intended outcomes. Derek Bok (2006) has rightly lamented a general "neglect of pedagogy" at all levels of higher education. He suggests that it may result in part from the fact that pedagogy refers by its definition to both the art *and* the science of teaching. Despite an increasing amount of research about learning and student outcomes in postsecondary education, there is a tendency to think that teaching is intuitive and cannot be taught. Those whose graduate degrees are in disciplines that are centrally occupied with investigating learning (composition studies, curriculum and instruction, and so on) are likely to see more coherence and potential for integration between interculturally effective teaching and their area of expertise. For others, however, there may not be an integrative element or alignment between disciplinary expertise and intentional pedagogy. Even in research on education, pedagogy is often an elusive element, so that "within journals focused on college teaching, little research or theory focuses on pedagogy or learning environment factors effective across cultural identities and norms" (Chávez, 2011, p. 54).

The task of developing effective intercultural pedagogy in relation to educational research can seem unmanageable in the midst of an already full plate. Amy Lee has seen this reality firsthand over the past decade as she mentored early career faculty at two large universities in programs designed to develop their teaching effectiveness in diverse contexts. The programs involved workshops on evidence-based instruction and learning research, monthly small team sessions, visits to other instructors' courses, and formal reflection on participants' beliefs about teaching and learning, influences that shaped their pedagogical theory and practice, and their lived experience as teachers. The two common themes that consistently emerged among participants in both undergraduate and graduate programs are also reflected in scholarship on teaching and learning as highly relevant to faculty interested in supporting intercultural competence.

First, a depth of expertise in disciplinary knowledge does not necessarily translate into effective teaching, regardless of whether the classroom consists of freshmen or doctoral students. As many of Amy's program participants have come to recognize, it is indispensable to *learn how to teach*. Yet many faculty members can reflect on their doctoral or early career experience and realize that they were provided minimal formal knowledge about learning or teaching, and did not receive substantial induction or training. This reflects Ladson-Billings's (1999) finding that "There is little to no systematic attention in doctoral programs to *teaching* preparation, to professionalizing *education*, and not subject matter." Many participants in Amy's programs followed a typical route by moving directly into teaching from the role of graduate research assistants to faculty members, and had no direct teaching experience when they walked into their first classroom. Others had been teaching assistants, responsible for grading records, labs, or discussion sections, but had not been responsible for developing syllabi, selecting content, designing activities and assignments, or planning regular course sessions.

A second theme emerged in the course of this experience when early career faculty repeatedly noted that the multiple obligations and competing pressures of their jobs made it difficult to commit time to acquiring knowledge and developing skills related to teaching. Even when participants had strong positive reactions to a particular instructional practice featured in one of our formal workshops, they often lacked awareness or understanding of how to adapt the practice to the specific context of their course. While institutional mission statements placed increasing emphasis on the importance of both effective teaching and diversity, the institutions did not invest the resources necessary to provide adequate time or training for faculty to fully develop a sense of expertise in relation to teachers. Yet over time, individual faculty can and do work effectively within that reality to seek out knowledge and professional development opportunities, form communities of practice, and engage in an ongoing process of exploration, experimentation, and reflection. Deliberate reflection and attention to pedagogy are core components of developing the capacity to engage diversity effectively. As shown earlier, the continued persistence of the mistaken assumption that learning happens from mere contact is in and of itself suggestive of a need to elaborate on the *how* element of fostering intercultural interactions in our classrooms (Kumagai and Lypson, 2009; Ladson-Billings, 1995a; Olson, Evans, and Shoenberg, 2007).

Faculty who want to engage diversity effectively must attend to the *how* of their classrooms. Particularly for those rooted in disciplinary traditions where a "sink or swim" approach to teaching is common, developing a more mindful pedagogy requires recognizing that there is mutual responsibility shared by instructor and students for students' learning. In other words, it requires noting, investigating, and responding to patterns that emerge in who sinks and who swims (such as attention in recent decade to disproportionate underrepresentation of females advancing in STEM [science, technology, engineering, math] fields and majors). A traditional, content-based pedagogy works well for some students whose learning styles are suited to the model of absorbing knowledge. It does not, however, work for all students, nor does it allow for or facilitate experiences key to intercultural competence development—opportunities to interact, practice, communicate, and reflect.

Developing intercultural pedagogy requires taking a mindful or critical stance so as to acknowledge the effects of our instruction and not only our intentions. In addition to a mindful or reflective stance, the creation of space for voices of students who can provide direct information regarding the quality and impact of their classroom experience is essential to informing subsequent refinements of our teaching (Day and others, 2004; Harper and Quaye, 2009). Langer (1997) argues that mindfulness is necessary in order to counteract learned "mindlessness" which is characterized by ". . . entrapment in old categories; by automatic behavior that precludes attending to new signals. . . . Being mindless, colloquially speaking, is like being on automatic pilot" (p. 4). Effective intercultural pedagogy requires that we reflect not only on how we present knowledge but also on how our assignments, course plans, lectures, and materials engage and support diverse learners.

An Integrated Framework for Intercultural Learning

Shifting from a content-based pedagogy to one that more deeply supports both disciplinary and intercultural learning requires a well-grounded model of how learning occurs. One such model that many intercultural scholars have found helpful is Kolb's (1984) classic learning cycle. Kolb (1984) argued that the learning process consists of four stages:

1. *Concrete experience*, usually in the form a direct encounter with a new person, perspective, or idea.
2. *Reflective observation* on the experience.
3. *Abstract conceptualization*, or the formulation and application of rules or theories to describe it.
4. *Active experimentation*—testing ways to modify the experience in the future.

The process described by Kolb is holistic and nonlinear, implying that one can enter at any one of the four steps. Individuals and groups have different preferences toward the elements of the learning cycle, and it is essential for instructors to incorporate experiences that fit the styles of all learners. In order to facilitate intercultural learning in an inclusive manner, we need to make sure that our classrooms include concrete experiences that challenge students to encounter diverse ideas, issues and people, reflective observation on their own intercultural learning in both formal and informal settings, abstract conceptualization to provide the information base for dealing with new diverse experiences, and multiple opportunities for active experimentation with diverse people and ideas (Lee, Williams, and Kilaberia, 2011).

As we showed earlier in the chapter, the landscape of college teaching in the United States is dominated by a heavy reliance on cognitive content or, to use Kolb's term, *abstract conceptualization*. Yet research on teaching and learning paints a clear picture of meaningful learning as a pendulum oscillating between experiencing and reflecting, acting and thinking, theorizing and experimenting. Immediate experience and active experimentation are central elements of the learning process. Collaborative learning techniques, for example, can introduce those elements into the classroom, providing both an impetus for learning and a site of creative practice.

The research literature abounds in evidence for the multiple benefits of active and reflective learning. In their study on pedagogy and social justice learning, Mayhew and DeLuca Fernández (2007) found that students learned more when they were exposed to classroom practices that encouraged reflection, peer interactions, and discussion about diversity. In their study, "Students who reflected on material, examined the material from different perspectives, and applied this knowledge to analyzing societal problems consistently gained a better understanding of themselves and issues related to diversity, regardless of course content" (p. 75). Kuszewski's (n.d.) review of several recent studies on learning in higher education, as well as her reflection on her own experience with formal schooling, led her to contend that teaching methods that focus on conveyance of content and memorization have a lasting effect on students' thinking and behavior, "making them more inclined towards linear thinking, and less prone to original, creative thinking" (p. 1). She argues that when pedagogy places students in a passive role, they are less motivated to engage in active thinking. She found that "once students have the answer, they aren't motivated to look for alternate solutions; errors are not rewarded when resulting from a potentially beneficial risk" (p. 2). In contrast, "Just by moving the students from passive observer to active participant, you are lighting a fire in the brain—making more connections across association areas, increasing plasticity, and enhancing learning" (p. 2).

Research findings increasingly correlate student outcomes to *how* faculty implement activities, content, and assignments, and not only to *what* activities, content, or assignments we use. Effective practices include purposefully embedding activities within the course context, connecting them to core learning outcomes, and signaling their value by assigning appropriate weight in the course grade. There is an overarching goal to promote cognitive complexity, enrich capacity to communicate effectively, and to value and utilize perspectives that differ from one's own (Gudykunst, 2005; Langer, 1989, 1997).

In the next section, we integrate Kolb's notion of learning as a pendulum of action and reflection with intercultural research presented in earlier chapters into concrete principles for an intercultural pedagogy.

Intercultural Pedagogical Principles

Faculty cannot mandate or manufacture intercultural competence *for* students (Wong, 2006). It is possible, however, to intentionally provide tools and classroom conditions that support students in their development. We turn now to outline core principles to inform the *how* of intercultural pedagogy. These have been developed through a synthesis of multiple areas of scholarship in an effort to provide a common framework for effective intercultural teaching. We have intentionally used the word *principle* to denote a conscious, explicit assumption that can inform course planning and design as well as classroom practice. In this section, we articulate and develop the principles; in the next two chapters, we implement and illustrate them within classroom contexts.

Principle 1: Intercultural Pedagogy Maximizes and Facilitates Purposeful Interactions

Interactions involve and impact the multiple domains of intercultural communication outlined in the preceding chapter. Most developmental theories suggest that social interaction is necessary to draw out the kind of cognitive disequilibrium that spurs growth (Hurtado, 2005). Interactions are not isolated activities that operate apart from cognitive stages of intercultural competence development. In fact, researchers have concluded that the frequency and quality of interactions with diverse perspectives and identities correlates to the development of general student learning and development outcomes, not just those associated with intercultural competence (Bowman, 2010b; Bruffee, 1999; Deardorff, 2009b; Denson and Chang, 2009; Hurtado, 2001).

In one study, students attributed more impact on their growth in critical thinking and problem solving to interaction with diverse peers than to exposure to a diverse curriculum (Hurtado, 2001). Nelson (1994) stated that "for many students, the acquisition of critical thinking skills may actually require collaborative learning" (p. 46). Each student brings a wealth of explicit and tacit models of how they believe information fits together, which are based on past experiences. Trying to make sense of new information, ideas, and perspectives, students try to fit these new experiences into their existent models or schemata (Nelson, 1994; Piaget, 1967). Working in diverse groups is one way students can interact with other mental models, which can lead to the disruption of students' current ways of thinking and the creation of discourse communities where different perspectives are valued and heard. Engaging diverse points of view facilitates not only critical thinking but also intercultural attitudes and skills, such as valuing diverse perspectives and managing one's own anxiety.

As students engage with one another and encounter differences in their fellow students' perspectives and epistemologies, it can at first be challenging for them to generate active dialogue or to reach productive consensus. Facilitated, purposeful opportunities to interact provide students with experience communicating, listening, and negotiating across complex cultural, experiential, and epistemological perspectives.

Principle 2: Intercultural Pedagogy Values the Assets Students Bring to the Classroom

When courses are intentionally structured to facilitate purposeful interaction related to course goals, it is possible to leverage the intellectual strengths and diversity of students and faculty rather than faculty alone. This requires "paying attention to the cultural differences diverse learners bring to the educational experience and how those cultural differences enhance the teaching and learning environment" (Danowitz and Tuitt, 2011, p. 43). Faculty who operate from this principle assume that there is value in students' insights and perspectives, and that soliciting students' insights and perspectives can contribute to deeper understanding and improve practice for reflective faculty (Langer, 1997; Quaye and Harper, 2009).

Given that individuals develop ways of knowing and communicating from multiple contexts such as family, home, and community, students will bring with them a range of assumptions and insights on course concepts and materials. To stimulate openness and critical thinking, it is important to support the capacity to make assumptions visible in order to critically engage them. Valuing students' lived experience and situated perspectives on course content gives their embodied knowledge the power to enrich or contest academic knowledge. For that reason, it is not a matter of passively enabling conversation and participation. As Goodman (1995) notes, bringing student perspectives into the classroom is a more complicated endeavor than telling stories for their own sake. In any given course, depending on the topic and other contextual factors, there will be different opportunities for facilitating dialogic, critical engagement of multiple participants' perspectives.

When asked why they don't incorporate intercultural views and perspectives into their courses, many instructors explain that they do not feel that they have the intercultural knowledge, resources, or time to adequately become proficient in what is perceived to be a separate discipline. This principle makes explicit that the instructor is not tasked with the impossible role of "intercultural knower" or source of intercultural knowledge. Rather, the instructor is responsible for facilitating the engagement of multiple perspectives in order to challenge students to wrestle with seemingly opposing ideas or to shift their frames of reference so as to consider alternative stances.

Moreover, courses that employ an active pedagogy provide designed space wherein students can express and develop the kind of cognitive complexity and communication skills that, if well-designed and facilitated, lead to the development of student intercultural competence. There is ample evidence that inviting experiential knowledge and insights, particularly in the form of narrative, can support empathic connection between students from diverse identity groups. Kumagai and Lypson (2009), among others, urge faculty to fully engage and maximize the potential of students' experience-based insights, not just inviting stories simply for "stories' sake." Rather, they argue that instructors can scaffold narrative-based contributions and experiential perspectives in relation to course goals and material in order to stimulate "critical reflection on one's own biases, privileges, and assumptions as well as acknowledgement of personal responsibility" (Boler, 1999, cited in Kumagai and Lypson, 2009, p. 785). The challenge for faculty is to implement "effective instructional use of personal and cultural knowledge while helping students reach beyond their cultural boundaries" (Banks, 1993, p. 8), a topic we will explore in more practical detail in the following two chapters.

Principle 3: Intercultural Pedagogy Balances Support and Dissonance

Facilitating student intercultural competence development requires affective, cognitive, and behavioral unsettling. Evidence from developmental psychology suggests that significant learning and personal growth can occur when one is exposed to unfamiliar experiences or ideas (Hurtado, 2001; Kumagai and Lypson, 2009; Piaget, 1985). The resulting individual learning may take the form of a self-reflective awareness as well as an ability to recognize and question the societal status quo (Kumagai and Lypson, 2009). It has been found that assuming different ways of viewing something enhances our interest, focus, learning, and communication (Langer, 1997). For that reason, discomfort and conflict play a significant role in "deepening the dialogic relating, expanding students' understanding of the issues that influence conflicts, and building students' capacity to work through disagreements and conflicts in productive ways" (Nagda and Gurin, 2007, p. 40).

Development cannot occur when persons stay in the same place, with the same interactive or intellectual patterns and behaviors. To support development beyond comfortable or familiar ways of perceiving or interacting, we must include acts of disruption within our planned learning environments. Such acts are intentionally designed to bring students into intercultural encounters that productively challenge—and possibly break—existing ways of thinking and behaving. When conflicts surface, it is important to learn how to interpret and respond in ways that position conflicts not "as a sign of failed dialogue; rather, they are opportunities for deeper learning. Similarly, working through conflicts is not automatically assumed to lead to a breach in the relationship; in fact, it is exactly because of working through conflicts that a deeper sense of community is developed" (Nagda and Gurin, 2007, p. 40).

At the same time, it is essential for instructors to balance challenge with support in a carefully designed learning environment. Encounters with dissonance around ideas or problems can work to break apart old notions and invite openness, but they also provoke an unavoidable increase in anxiety that can ultimately cause one to strengthen one's defenses and become entrenched in prejudice. The ability to manage anxiety is a crucial component of intercultural competence (Gudykunst, 1998, 2002), yet one that few students possess when they arrive at college. It is the responsibility of the instructor to mindfully control the level of anxiety in the classroom, and to model to students how anxiety can be managed on a personal level. It has been demonstrated that reducing anxiety about interactions with others has powerful effects on the tone and outcomes of interaction; it is also known as the most effective mediator for decreasing prejudice in relating to others, much more powerful, in fact, than increasing knowledge about them (Pettigrew and Tropp, 2008).

It is not possible to predict what will propel support or dissonance for individual students, and so it is necessary to consider diversity in the design of an environment. For example, in describing a curriculum for cultural competency development among law students, Hartley and Petrucci (2004) observed that for some students, a safe environment is one where people are calm and do not raise their voices. For others, a safe environment is one where anger and conflict can surface freely. Recognition of these differences is a critical part of intercultural competence development because dissonance can be experienced and expressed in different ways, as the law students in Hartley and Petrucci's research demonstrated. When engaged effectively and mindfully, dissonance and responses to it can be powerful tools in further exploring and supporting seemingly conflicting ideas and the methods of communicating about them.

Developing Intercultural Pedagogy—A Continuous Process That Happens Over Time

As noted earlier in this chapter, it is helpful in thinking about pedagogy in general and intercultural pedagogy in particular to remember that its development follows a similar course as the development of intercultural competence itself. Learning to teach effectively and learning to teach in ways that support intercultural competence development are processes that rely on acquiring knowledge, experiencing interactions in a "live" and dynamic context, and engaging in reflective practice that facilitates the ability to adapt to shifting and particular conditions and factors of any given course—such as the number of students, student demographics, level of course, and physical classroom space. The goal is to have a flexible set of tools and concepts that instructors can adopt and adapt across diverse contexts, as well as the ability to assess the effectiveness of the instruction in relation to the outcomes.

The continuous nature of pedagogical development encourages us to abandon the idea that professors are supposed to have already mastered teaching, and realize instead that, in the words of Ladson-Billings (1999), teaching is an "unfinished" profession (p. 238). Effective practitioners are constantly learning, testing, and refining approaches and practice. Most faculty members are regularly adjusting and responding to changes that impact their teaching and are outside of their control. Fundamental conditions of our teaching are inevitably in flux, both from one term to another and over the course of our careers. Student populations change; new content and skills are emphasized as academic majors and requirements shuffle; new technologies are available or even imposed; course sizes change; and institutions develop new learning outcomes and educational goals. Most models of faculty development—especially those whose roots are in critical pedagogy, feminist pedagogy, and equity pedagogy—emphasize the importance of an intentional reflective process that cycles between action, critique, assessment, and adaptation.

Ideally, instructors have access to institutional or discipline-based professional development opportunities, such as workshops or programs offered by centers for teaching, or local conferences on teaching and learning. Even without institutional resources, instructors can convene with colleagues to provide deeper support for implementing effective pedagogy. Regular informal discussions about teaching, for instance, among a community of practitioners would serve to develop a network of support and shared expertise. Peer course visits that are used as occasions for dialogue, rather than for evaluation or assessment purposes, can also be fruitful. When colleagues visit one another's courses and discuss insights, questions, and challenges, they have the opportunity to develop formal knowledge together that bridges authentic sites of practice and practitioner knowledge (Gallagher and Lee, 2008; Stenberg and Lee, 2002).

Classrooms as Privileged Spaces

Developing an effective intercultural pedagogy necessitates acknowledging that whether or not one intends or is aware of it, "our values get embedded into our courses through how we structure curriculum, class time" (Gair and Mullins, 2001, p. 26). Harper and Quaye (2009), citing Gurin, Dey, Hurtado, and Gurin (2002) and Light (2001), noted that despite evidence that meaningful intercultural interaction enhances learning and development, we continue to teach in what is believed to be culturally neutral ways, and we thus we fail to maximize the opportunities available in our classes. Any pedagogy that seeks to sponsor intercultural interaction needs to take a deliberate, reflective stance that resists the assumption that teachers and students enter an equally "safe" space inside of our classes, a space where our deeply held beliefs are held in abeyance. The issue isn't whether we choose to bring ideology into the classroom because it is already there (Ellsworth, 1989; Gore, 1993; Lee, 2001). All pedagogies are informed by sociopolitical contexts and in turn enact understandings about how knowledge is constructed, what counts as valid knowledge, and who can create or contribute to knowledge. As Clifford (1991) concluded in his discussion of debates about the politicization of writing instruction, any teachers "who ask students to rehearse particular . . . rituals in the classroom impose an ideological agenda, admitted or not . . . of course, since ideology thrives on anonymity, we think of our appointed tasks as commonsensical, not ideological" (pp. 45–46). Whether we subscribe to a humanist, feminist, or sage on the stage pedagogy, we must recognize and be accountable for the impact of our pedagogy for diverse learners.

Composition and English studies scholars sometimes refer to the classroom or teaching as a "text" (Christensen, 1989; Lee, 2001; Stenberg and Lee, 2002; VanDeWeghe and Reid, 2000). The concept of the classroom as a "text" draws attention to the fact that a classroom (like a poem or policy document) is not a static or universal entity but rather a negotiation between multiple participants who bring distinct lenses to the text, and who will emerge with distinct and possibly multiple competing interpretations and impressions. In a classroom, the instructor and the students are active negotiators in the outcomes of a course (Ellsworth, 1989; Gore, 1993; Stewart, 2008). The course curriculum and content, like the poem, do not exist in a vacuum and cannot be encountered as a "free" or blank space that eliminates biography, historical context, existing knowledge, or training. Wildman (1995) cautioned against assuming that a classroom can simply be suspended space, uninfluenced by broader contexts and lived experience. Whether in regards to a poem, a formula, or a classroom, our experience and interpretation of the "text" is inevitably influenced by the context we bring to it, by our past experiences, existing knowledge, assumptions, and values. Faculty and students, of course, also enter a course with particular expectations, educational histories, and expectations. This requires instructors to be mindful of the multiple, fluid identities and preconceptions of others that impact collaboration and inter-action. An instructor who is seeking to effectively engage diversity will acknowledge this reality rather than ignore or minimize it.

We must not believe that in the absence of obvious or visible unfair treat-ment, all individuals are similarly situated in the classrooms or institution. Tatum (1992) argues that, in fact, we should assume that prejudice exists in any given class as a result of the cultural stereotypes we are *all* exposed to sys-tematically. The realization that prejudice is unavoidably present in classrooms is particularly relevant with reference to race and racial identity. According to Wildman (1995), "if we say race plays no part, then the invisible system of white privilege will inevitably continue" (p. 91). Social constructions of identity enter learning environments and impact the relations and dynamics within them in a variety of ways, one of which is the phenomenon of stereotype threat. Stereotype threat enters the picture when "societal stereotypes about groups can influence the intellectual functioning and identity development of indi-vidual group members" (Steele, 1997, p. 613). Negative stereotypes, even when not actively or visible validated or perpetuated in a particular social space, are deeply internalized and accumulative for individual group mem-bers, and threat of stereotypes can act as an "achievement barrier." In partic-ular, the threat of negative perceptions of academic ability based on social group status leads to increased stressors and decreased academic performance (Rypisi, Malcom, and Kim, 2009). Even positive associations with a social group (such as female students being strong collaborators) have negative con-sequences because they deny the individuality and complexity of a person (Tatum, 1992). Various perceptions and assumptions about group identity, whether positive or negative, obviously saturate and impact intergroup inter-actions in the classroom.

Even if a given instructor is not actively reinforcing normative stereotypes regarding the aptitude of particular students based on membership in a group, the internalization of those stereotypes by students can influence their per-formance and self-efficacy in class. In other words, to not perpetuate or act on stereotypes in one's class is not the same as actively disrupting them so as to engineer a supportive, inclusive space. The next two chapters elaborate on particular practices and considerations that can support the design and implementation of classroom practice that mindfully supports intercultural interaction.

Conclusion

Every course provides opportunities for students to engage in interactions that elicit the cognitive and relational work that is fundamental to intercultural competence. Successfully harnessing these opportunities cannot happen without a commitment on the part of the instructor to ongoing development and to the three principles outlined in this chapter.

While classrooms provide authentic contexts for engaging diversity, instructors must decide how best to leverage this potential as there is no "one size fits all" model for this work. The final two chapters focus on implementing educational practices that value and invite communication across difference and facilitate opportunities for intercultural communication and collaboration so as to maximize the classroom as a site of engaging diversity.

Engaging Diversity Through Course Design and Preparation

W E HAVE ARGUED THAT A CLASSROOM designed to foster intercultural competence is characterized less by its content and more by the ways in which it is taught and how it engages students in the learning process. It requires a pedagogy that incorporates available resources (such as the curriculum, instructional practices, and the knowledge students bring to class) to support students' development of a toolkit of behaviors, knowledge, and awareness that enable their intercultural competence. In these final chapters, we focus on pedagogical actions that are informed by intercultural pedagogy. We use the term *action* in reference to Kumagai and Lypson's (2009) concept of educational praxis, which is defined as action informed by an overarching theoretical framework. The concept of educational praxis signals the importance of a dialectic relationship between theory and practice, and reflection and action. It highlights the continuous and interactive nature of intercultural pedagogy and the reality that practitioners develop it over time, through processes of mindful adaption and adjustment in response to specific learning contexts.

The theoretical framework for engaging diversity through intercultural pedagogy was established in the first three chapters. We intentionally defined diversity to include not only race and ethnicity but the range of visible and invisible factors that interact to form individual and social constructions of identity. Intercultural pedagogy intentionally targets cognitive, affective, and behavioral growth processes that contribute to developing the capacity to "consciously value complex and integrated differences" in ourselves and others (Chávez, Guido-DiBrito, and Mallory, 2003, p. 453). We articulated three foundational principles for intercultural pedagogy based on synthesis of research that focuses on diversity and cultural competency. These principles reflect the core premise of engaging diversity: students bring relevant knowledge and experiences to the classroom, and diverse perspectives enhance student development (Arkoudis and others, 2010; Danowitz and Tuitt, 2011; Deardorff, 2009b; Sheets, 2009; Smith, 2010). The principles should be embedded in the approach to teaching and manifest in the structure of the classroom, selection and design of course components, and interactions with students.

These last two chapters elaborate on the actions that emerge from this theoretical framework, focusing on the "how" of the three intercultural pedagogy principles. We have organized these chapters according to two common stages faculty undergo in relation to teaching: course preparation and classroom management. While these stages do not always occur sequentially or separately, looking at them as component parts will help to generate a reflective stance on whether they are operating in a mutually supportive continuum. This chapter focuses on incorporating the intercultural pedagogical principles during the stage of course design and preparation. Mindful and thorough preparation enhances the experience and learning outcomes of both students and instructors, but even the most careful course design is only the prologue to actual classroom reality. Therefore, the final chapter turns to the second stage of implementation and management, and proposes strategies to draw on when implementing intercultural pedagogy in real time with real students present.

Incorporating Intercultural Pedagogical Principles into Course Design

All faculty are tasked with some degree of course design, which refers to the elements of the class that one can plan and prepare for before students come into the classroom. Each course requires a measure of preparation and production of key components, including a schedule, assigned readings and materials, a syllabus, and learning activities. These components convey the priorities and goals of the course as well as instructor expectations for students' participation and effort.

Intercultural pedagogy should inform the approach to core content, learning activities, and the design of the classroom environment. In other words, it is important for multiple dimensions of a course to be in alignment in reflecting the importance of engaging diversity (Arkoudis and others, 2010; Danowitz and Tuitt, 2011; Marin, 2000). It is not sufficient to merely adopt an instructional method without attention to the broader context and in which it used (McGee Banks and Banks, 1995; Sheets, 2005). To achieve intended outcomes, instructors must reflect on the extent to which course components work in sync with one another. Without such reflection, we run the risk of communicating confusing and mixed messages to our students. For instance, we may signal value for active learning in the syllabus by heavily weighing collaborative work in the course grade, but fail to provide structures that facilitate interaction, or to leave adequate time for its implementation in class. In a similar scenario, crowded class schedules may results in a focus on conveying or "covering" key content in spite of a stated emphasis on supporting students' opportunities to apply and integrate the content.

Mayhew and DeLuca Fernández (2007) point to findings in the literature that identify three pedagogical practices as effective in contributing to social justice-oriented learning outcomes, which we postulate as helpful for faculty who aim to support intercultural competence development:

1. Provide opportunities for perspective-taking and reflection.
2. Structure opportunities for collaboration and interaction with diverse peers.
3. Provide opportunity for application of knowledge.

Based on an extensive review of contemporary literature, we also suggest the following two practices as essential in the context of college classrooms:

1. Explicitly identify relevant intercultural skills, behaviors, and attitudes.
2. Establish an environment that supports engaging diversity.

In the next section, we develop these practices in relation to the stage of course design, and provide examples of course components that are in alignment with the three principles of intercultural pedagogy. Given that many courses have existing requirements attached to them by programs or institutional mandates, it is understood that instructors will need to reflect on how they might adapt the elements of intercultural pedagogy to the particular context of their course.

Provide Opportunities for Reflection and Perspective Taking

Whether or not the institutional context enables an instructor to choose the textbook or readings, one can consider how to approach the required materials from multiple perspectives, how to frame students' lived experiences as relevant to course content, and design opportunities to challenge students to think critically about their own and others' perspectives (Anderson, 2008; Nelson Laird and Engberg, 2009). One way to signal the importance of students' active engagement is by incorporating conditional language into the syllabus, reading selections, and one's own communication with students. Conditional language, such as *could be, observes,* or *possibilities include,* signals that there is intellectual room for students to interact with content and discuss concepts and ideas. It also communicates that disciplinary knowledge is enriched by active participation in interpretations or experimentation (Langer, 1997; Richards, 2003).

An example of the use of conditional language is found in *Understanding the American Promise,* a textbook designed for U.S. history survey courses (Roark and others, 2011). In this text, conditional language is used to foster students' longitudinal skill development while communicating core disciplinary content. Although the text focuses on skills that are relevant to historiography, many of those are transferable to intercultural competence, for example, observation, interpretation, perspective taking, and the influence of sociocultural context on historical interpretation. For instance, when the authors pose the question, "Is it fair to describe the American people as 'isolationist' prior to America's entry into World War I? Why or why not?" (Roark and others, 2011, p. 625), they do not frame it as either absolute or rhetorical. Rather, the question invites students to use skills of analysis and observation in the process of producing complex historical interpretations supported by evidence. Because the question invites multiple interpretations, it provides a subsequent opportunity for critical engagement with different perspectives through a facilitated dialogue among students and the instructor and a space that is inclusive of different forms of evidence or experience.

Faculty can also invite and model cognitive complexity by choosing to provide a frame of reference or explicit context for assigned reading. Rather than simply presenting a listing of books and other instructional resources to students without contextual commentary, instructors could instead foreground the rationale for the selection of particular texts. The instructor can explain that she or he intentionally chose to introduce students to dissonant views on a given topic, divergent approaches to inquiry and interpretation, and multiple constructions of knowledge among scholars in the discipline.

For example, an instructor might provide students with an initial introductory bibliography of texts that are considered core, canonical works in the discipline. However, the bibliography could be framed by an introductory statement, included with the initial bibliography, that explicitly references that and why students will encounter disagreement and even conflicting interpretations of events, persons, and evidence. This serves to make explicit the rich complexity of disciplinary discourse and to make visible that multiple approaches are part of intellectual inquiry and that reconciliation is a process and not an assumption. Students can then be invited to actively extend the bibliography by locating, examining, and annotating relevant texts they could submit for review by the instructor and peers for potential inclusion and subsequent discussion in class. Inviting students to contribute to the ongoing establishment of a "canon" encourages critical thinking and encourages an inquisitive approach to disciplinary content.

As discussed in the preceding chapter, Kolb's (1984) model of learning suggests that active encounters with new ideas must be combined with frequent opportunities to reflect on the concepts themselves as well as one's own way of relating to them. Meaningful intercultural learning requires a pendulum of external engagement and internal reflection. One way to facilitate reflection is through writing assignments about students' experience with difference in the classroom. Such assignments provide instructors with key information about students' levels of anxiety and help structure future assignments in a way that prevents an individual from passing the dangerous threshold where learning is blocked (Gudykunst, 2005). Student writing also provides feedback on what the course is accomplishing as far as developing intercultural competence and guiding how intercultural competence relates to the course of study.

Structure Opportunities for Collaboration and Interaction with Diverse Peers

Design Purposeful Activities and Assignments That Engage Diversity. As established by research reviewed in previous chapters, interactions that "bring diverse students together in meaningful, civil discourse to learn from each other" (Gurin, Nagda, and Lopez, 2004, p. 32) are a critical component of classrooms that engage diversity. Interactions necessitate communication and cooperative skills that are foundational to intercultural competence development. It is important to signal in the syllabus that interactions are a substantive and important component of the course by providing a structure that prompts students to go beyond superficial discussion. Furthering intercultural outcomes also requires that instructors not only provide frequent opportunity for interaction, but that these are well designed and purposeful. Research suggests that people tend to experience their interactions with others as more positive when cooperation is positively valued and seen as necessary for the achievement of mutual goals (Allport, 1954). Purposeful interactions that engage diversity can be facilitated through incorporating collaborative learning techniques, such as goal-oriented small-group work with diverse participation. Without such purposeful design, we may provide space for intercultural "encounters," but those may in fact facilitate effects that are directly opposed to the intended or desired outcomes (Hurtado, 2001; Otten, 2003). Instead of fostering a greater understanding, in fact, "they can even reinforce stereotypes and prejudices" (Hurtado, 2001, p. 15). A rich array of literature provides guidance for instructors related to cooperative and collaborative learning and their use in culturally diverse settings. Such literature includes evidence-based models and sources that contain relevant nuances of implementation. We do not have the space to adequately review or present the richness of this literature, but we provide a few references for those seeking a more in-depth understanding and guidance (Bruffee, 1999; King, 2002; Sampson and Cohen, 2001; Wenger and Snyder, 2000).

Collaborative learning activities are uniquely suited for the goal of fostering intercultural competence by supporting students' interaction with classmates and content. Structured opportunities to engage with diverse peers in working toward a common purpose can help counteract the tendency to "retreat into homogeneous space of comfort" (Arkoudis and others, 2010; Milem, Chang, and Antonio, 2005). Research demonstrates that students engaged in diverse cooperative learning groups improve their interaction skills with students from different backgrounds, and they are much more likely to report cross-racial friendships outside these groups (Hurtado, 2001).

Collaborative learning can occur in informal groups that work on a problem together for the duration of one class period, or formal term projects that span the entire semester. Examples of specific types of group work include collaborative project work, peer review of student writing, or consensual response to lectures (Bruffee, 1999). Informal collaborative activities are usually short in duration and used to ensure active learning. They might be used, for example, to break up a lecture with peer exchanges that require students to organize, explain, and otherwise cognitively process their learning (Johnson, Johnson, and Smith, 1998).

Research on collaborative learning dispels the illusion that collaborative activities are simply a matter of having students work in groups with little support from the instructor. Studies have found that "it is rare for collaborating learners to engage spontaneously in effective interaction or match their type of interaction to the task at hand without some form of explicit prompting or other guidance by their teachers" (King, 2008, p. 75). In fact, research has shown that, even when given instructions to work collaboratively on a task, learners generally tend to interact with each other at a concrete level in a specific step-by-step manner rather than at an abstract and mindful level unless the teacher intercedes with explicit guidance in how to interact (Bruffee, 1999; King, 2008; Webb, Ender, and Lewis, 1986). One student's description of a collaborative activity early in the term illustrates the typical awkwardness that characterizes initial group work and that can remain if instructors do not intentionally facilitate and structure collaboration. The student wrote that as students moved their seats together, they were aware of being "strangers to each other," with different cultural backgrounds and a "different way of thinking."

He found that first discussion to be "really tough and uncomfortable, people kind of felt constrained to speak up. I saw some of us looking at the ground and being shy, some of us were staring at others and [one student] looked like he has some expectation to hear from others and one person seemed already decide to do the job on his own."

Observing students interact in small groups in the first week can help instructors tailor subsequent activities to support communication and collaboration. Informal observations will provide information about interpersonal dynamics: Who feels entitled to speak? Who assumes authority? Who struggles to be heard? For example, in the initial few class meetings during small-group work, an instructor may note that students in several groups are having difficulty listening to other group members. They may be interrupting or doing something other than listening. Instructors' observations can be augmented by inviting students to practice reflective assessment on the group dynamics and roles: What factors contributed to or inhibited students' communication and learning? What might the student do differently? What do they wish group members might do differently? How can the instructor support future group communications and collaboration? Making reflection a visible part of collaboration is important given that learning to work and communicate cooperatively is a process that develops over time and practice. The more transparency provided, through actively discussing and reflecting on collaborative experiences, the more readily students can learn to prepare for and contribute to their groups.

Allocate Time So as to Signal the Value of Interactions. Allocating adequate time for purposeful interactions and structuring them into the class schedule may require modest or significant shifts in the way that faculty utilize classroom time. Time allocation is a critical component in courses that are designed to support students' intercultural competence development. The capacity to create new categories, develop openness to new information, and analyze and interpret more than one perspective, for example, requires time to practice and reflect (Gudykunst, 2005; Langer, 1989, 1997). If there is rhetorical attention to the value of collaborative learning in a syllabus, but class sessions are not organized so as to facilitate time and class structure for this to occur substantively, there is little chance that students will have the opportunity to develop their competency.

As one of our students said, "mixing it up" in class by changing normal patterns of classroom structure can not only signal and elicit openness to multiple ways of knowing but reinforce the message that students are understood to be capable of contributing to the knowledge-building enterprise of the class. Rather than beginning each class with a lecture format, an instructor can vary the pattern by opening with small-group discussions framed by a question that is posed or by presenting a video or music clip or an image that will provoke interpretations and discussion related to the material being discussed in that class session. While this may seem simple, it is another opportunity to reinforce alignment between the stated goals and the design of the course.

An example from a class taught by Robert Poch, one of the authors of this monograph, offers another illustration of how time can be purposefully allocated to balance the presentation of content, opportunity for students to engage with complex core concepts, and the practice of intercultural skills and behaviors. First, students viewed the short film *Underground* (Dehert and Lagos, 2003). Because the film is intentionally provocative in its depiction of race, gender, and class, students often form immediate and fixed opinions about what is happening in the film and find it challenging to consider alternative interpretations. Second, students were asked to take brief reflective notes to document their perceptions of what was happening in the film. Third, students were asked to pair off with a student that they do not know and to participate in several exercises. They began by taking turns listening to their partner's interpretation of the film without interrupting except to ask clarifying questions. Then, the students who listened repeated to their partner what they heard their partner say, checking if their interpretation of that person's comments and observations was accurate without expressing evaluative judgments about the partner's views.

The goal of the course session was to grapple with the concept and influence of social construction of identity as central to social events as well as to the nature of constructing historical accounts. Rather than show the film and lecture about its relevance to the course or follow up with a Socratic method-oriented activity, the instructor sought to involve students in practicing skills and behaviors relevant to the academic content and intercultural competence. The activity as designed and facilitated provided a space for skill development related to actively listening, participating in dialogue, and the ability to accurately represent other perspectives without first interjecting or disagreeing. The exercise and the film were debriefed in the large group, with the instructor continuing to model and support active listening, observing, and interpreting. Students often commented that they became aware of aspects of the film that they had not observed on their own, and that their interpretations were modified, informed, or enhanced by listening to the observations and interpretations of their partner and by the responsibility to accurately record their partner's perspective before interjecting, disagreeing, or augmenting it.

From this activity, students were led through the difficult process of truly listening to another individual—a vital skill to understanding and relating to diverse others. To be able to truly listen to another individual involves several subskills, such as suspending judgment and listening without interrupting. The activity broke down the process into several manageable and explicit steps: (1) listen without speaking; (2) respond without inserting one's opinion, just what they heard; (3) offer one's own thoughts and perspectives; and (4) reflect upon the process and how it added to one's own interpretation and perspectives on the topic. The last guided step, reflection upon the skill being developed in relation to the topic, is critical to a student's cognitive development (that is, complexity of thought or critical thinking).

Incorporate Purposeful Opportunities to Apply Experiential Knowledge

Instructors can engage diversity by giving students opportunities to connect their affective experiences and cognitive frames, using their experiential knowledge as an instrument of critical inquiry that can be applied to course content. As suggested in the intercultural pedagogical principle of valuing the assets students bring to the classroom, it is important to provide space to assert and author their own identity.

One of the ways to incorporate experience-based knowledge in the classroom is integrating narrative into the classroom. Narrative inquiry can engage students' affective as well as cognitive domains, foster perspective taking, and enhance empathic connections with others (Hoskins, 1998; King, 2002; Turniansky and others, 2009). Inclusion of opportunities to engage experiential knowledge as a site for critical inquiry lays bare the "necessary contextual contours to the seeming 'objectivity' of positivist perspectives" (Ladson-Billings, 1999, p. 213). Stories are a powerful way of showing how the reality we perceive is shaped by our backgrounds and experiences, and subsequent dialogue "allows the participants to actually live the experience of being part of a diverse learning community" (Turniansky and others, 2009, p. 42).

One example of this is an assignment frequently used at the beginning of a course that involves the sharing of "cultural artifacts." Versions of this assignment (biographical object; learning narrative) may be familiar to instructors, as it has been featured in journals on pedagogy as an effective assignment for fostering interpersonal knowledge and setting the stage for interactions in a course (Lee, Williams, and Kilaberia, 2011). Students are asked to select an object from their lives that reflects an aspect of their cultural identity. The assignment requires them to write about the object (for example, describe it in detail; explicate its meaning; account for why they selected it and how it was associated with meaning in relation to some aspect of their cultural identity). Students then present their cultural artifacts to one another (this can occur in small or whole-class groups).

This assignment can be varied easily to adapt to a particular class and works well early in the term because it enables students to proactively establish a sense of their identity for one another and support the development of rapport and builds a basis for future group cooperative learning. In Robert Poch's implementation of this assignment, he required students to write summaries of what they heard from at least three other students. Their summaries were collected by Poch so as to validate their importance as meaningful, legitimate work, and students were asked to respond to the questions: What have you learned about the student and his/her culture through the story that he/she shared? What was the most important piece of information that the student shared with you today? This created both accountability and a record of three other students that they could then use as reference points for future interactions.

Students demonstrate respect for their peers by listening intently to each story as it is told. This is confirmed by the inclusion of the summary component and its review by the instructor. Overall, the activity helps to establish and enact trust, building relationships that prove useful in subsequent classroom exchanges of cultural information and communication. Instructors who adapt similar assignments often observe that students refer later in the course to this assignment, reporting that it enabled them to affirmatively present some aspect of their identity or experience, and that it supported future points of connection between students and to content. As one student described:

> I do wish that at times all my classes created somewhat of a unit like this one because it helps build a bit of a relationship with everyone in the class, and the story behind the object gives a lot of information about one person, which I think that this help[ed] everyone to create a trust between one another.

This assignment could be tailored to a variety of contexts simply by changing the subject. For example, a colleague who teaches a course on ethnography shifts the assignment to serve as an early induction into the method of participant observation research, though it also facilitates interpersonal knowledge among students premised on each student having space to determine how they want to present an aspect of their experience and identity. In a course on gender and popular culture, Amy Lee had students bring a token, object, or image that reflected their earliest direct memory of "gendering." The assignment was structured in ways similar to what is described above, leaving room for students to determine what they wanted to disclose, and serving to facilitate connections between theoretical and empirical research being studied in the course and students lived experiences in family and cultural contexts. Given the highly visible ways gender norms operate in a group setting as well as the likelihood that there will be deeply held beliefs about gender and both inclinations toward and resistance to contesting those, the assignment helps students enter the course work from where they are while pushing them to begin critically unpacking some core concepts. Students evoked this early assignment frequently throughout the semester in ways that indicated how it formed a basis for interpersonal knowledge among peers, as well as serving to mark the progression of their understandings about the intersections of popular culture, gender, and identity through the course.

There are many opportunities to incorporate biographical information into a particular class. It may happen periodically, and formally or informally, in a learning journal and regular reflective paper, or in small-group guided activities that invite students to connect experience-based knowledge to course concepts and texts. In any way it is done, making space for critical engagement with experiential knowledge, not just stories for stories' sake, is important to connect affective experiences and cognitive frames in a way that propels intercultural competence.

The outcome of applying experiential knowledge is illustrated in a reflection by a student who found that the lived experiences of her classmates and roommate prompted her to reflect on her attitude toward a social group she had not previously validated. Her reflection is also illustrative of the strong interdependence of the affective and cognitive domains of learning:

> While I have always been taught to appreciate and respect people who are different, I have never really learned to accept people who are considered to be "normal," or similar to the typical person living in the United States. When I have talked about diversity in school or with my family and friends in the past, little or no validation has been given to the culture of a white, American Christian. In . . . class, I was surprised by the number of people who discussed the importance of Christianity in their lives. My roommate, who is also a close friend of mine, is a white, Christian American, and she's my first close friend who fits that description. Recently, we were talking about religion and politics, and I came to realize that I had never really learned to consider the most common opinions or practices that are found in this country. Because I have so much respect and friendship with my roommate already, her opinions were really important to me and for the first time I really heard out someone coming from her perspective. I think that this had a lot to do with the course, where I have learned that diversity applies to everybody, not just the people who are considered to be "different" from the norm.

Another student describes the process by which exposure to the experiential knowledge of classmates increased his sensitivity toward others in his life who face similar challenges:

> *After watching the presentation from Maria and Mateo, I thought a lot about how people stereotype people. One thing that happened to my friend about a month ago is a great example. . . . I was hanging out with a bunch of my college friends and they are all white except for one girl, Sophie, who is Chinese. I made some comment similar to, "It's OK, we are all white here." Sophie spoke up and said, "I'm not" and laughed. I apologized and she said it happened all of the time. I talked to her later in private and found out that it really does bother her because she is proud of being Chinese but since she has a lot of white friends, she is just thought of as one of them. If I hadn't been in this class, I don't think I would have thought about this incident as deeply as I did.*

Of course, the mere act of creating space for experiential knowledge or narratives about lived experience is not enough to foster identification or further development of one's intercultural competence. It is important to reflect on how these contributions are incorporated into and made relevant in relation to the course goals (Kumagai and Lypson, 2009) so as to not only stimulate empathic connection, but also critical reflection on one's own frame of reference, including biases, privileges, and assumptions (Boler, 1999, cited in Kumagai and Lypson, 2009). The challenge for teachers is to make "effective instructional use of personal and cultural knowledge while helping students reach beyond their cultural boundaries" (Banks, 1993, p. 12).

Explicitly Identify Relevant Intercultural Skills, Behaviors, and Attitudes

In the process of integrating intercultural pedagogy into a course, it is important to reflect on whether core components are designed so as to consistently and explicitly represent how and why intercultural competence skills and interactions are substantive features of the course. For example, a syllabus provides students with an introduction to course goals, key concepts to be investigated, and priorities for learning and assessment. The syllabus also communicates to students, whether implicitly or explicitly, what they can expect of the course environment and the relationships that will be established between students and instructors, students and their peers, and students with the content of the course.

Learning goals related to intercultural competence can be reinforced in many different parts of the syllabus, including the course description, course objectives, assignments, and assessments. The way the syllabus is structured can make definitive statements about the goals and assignments that support engaging diversity. It can emphasize the importance of reflection and perspective taking, the application of knowledge, multiple perspectives, or the value and means by which students' experiential knowledge will interact with course content (Anderson, 2008; Nelson Laird and Engberg, 2009). It is also helpful to include an explicit statement about the course environment and the qualities of participation that are considered integral to the learning process. For instance, behaviors and attitudes such as respect, active listening, tolerance for ambiguity, or patience with dissonance can be identified as intentional and expected components of students' participation and learning.

For example, a lower-division biology course syllabus would likely include information about the assigned readings, describe the form and weight of exams, identify key concepts and knowledge or learning outcomes, and describe how the lab component will work. This basic information may remain in a revised syllabus that integrates intercultural principles in the course design. The revised syllabus would explicitly mention intercultural skills and behaviors that are relevant to this particular course, such as openness to new information, or observing and analyzing before interpreting and evaluating. It would provide a description of how those skills and behaviors would be demonstrated, valued, and assessed in course learning activities. A section on the lab component might include an explanation on the value of collaboration in the process of scientific investigation and interpretation, which would be further reflected in the design of assignments or assessments that support purposeful collaboration.

In some contexts, particular courses are obligated to feature course content and possibly assignments that are determined programmatically rather than by the individual instructors. There is still opportunity to incorporate intercultural pedagogy into the syllabus by using language that establishes how the course will invite students to play an active role in the conversation and learning process, as opposed to signaling that communication will primarily be one-way, from instructor to students. For example, if a syllabus states the importance of cooperative learning, but then goes on to include a class schedule that features only the content to be covered, it will signal that content coverage is the focal point and other aspects of the course design are merely an afterthought.

Establish an Environment That Supports Engaging Diversity

How students view peers in class and the ease they feel in contributing, critiquing, and considering ideas with each other have direct implications for their level of engagement with diversity and their development of both cognitive and affective diversity competencies. According to Gurin, Dey, Hurtado, and Gurin (2002), it is essential to accommodate different perspectives yet challenge students to move beyond the comfort of membership in a homogeneous group in order to create productive learning. Instructors know that each semester the manner in which students initially interact is unpredictable and highly varied. Building a respectful classroom environment begins with modeling the skills we also ask of our students and laying down the ground rules of classroom interaction. Instructors may choose in the first class session to invite students into a discussion of the qualities and behaviors that help build a learning environment that they will find safe and engaging. Actively establishing a respectful classroom environment is essential to supporting purposeful and substantive interactions among students.

Allport (1954) noted that when people from different social groups interact and work together, the outcomes are more likely to be positive if all participants have equal status. This conclusion resonates with Gudykunst's (2005) finding that people are less likely to experience anxiety in interactions with others if they feel that they have some power in their relationships with strangers. Students bring different levels of perceived status and empowerment to the classroom, depending on the language they speak at home, the color of their skin, the culture and religion they identify with, and many other factors. Many pedagogical theories, including culturally relevant pedagogy, equity pedagogy, and critical pedagogy, establish the inadequacy of assuming that good intentions on the part of an instructor will yield equal status or opportunity for students (Brown-Jeffy and Cooper, 2011; Ellsworth, 1989; Ladson-Billings, 1995a). We must repeatedly ask ourselves who is invited to talk and whose talk is valued. It is essential that instructors actively support the implementation of an inclusive environment beyond including ground rules or a values statement in a syllabus. While a useful starting point, instructors must be proactive in helping students put into practice the conditions that facilitate a learning environment that supports students' ability to contribute and participate, and that accommodates diverse communication styles.

For example, early in a course, instructors can ask students to generate collective agreements about the behaviors and values that would constitute a positive and effective learning environment. Depending on the size of the class, this could happen in small groups or large, and students can be given prompts that sponsor discussion about the factors that stimulate, support, or inhibit their participation and engagement in the classroom. In one course class, a student referred back to this activity at the end of term in a learning journal, pointing to its significance in setting a stage for the semester:

> *We were and still are able to show our abilities to do those things that we spoke about on that first day. We . . . respect each other's opinions and don't hold different opinions against each other and work as a team when we are put together, whether we know one another or not. . . . We really delight in talking about it and having all of the discussions we do in class. This is part of the respect that we all have for each other and our opinions. We are all courteous towards each other during discussion and can speak freely.*

Another option is to have students do a short reflective writing on formative experiences, positive or negative, in educational settings, followed by asking them to reflect on behaviors and qualities that impacted their involvement and the quality of their learning. This can be debriefed in the large group and facilitated toward consensus building about guidelines for classroom practices that support students' engagement. Overall, this is an intentional and active means of demonstrating that learning is going to be a collective endeavor and thus the quality and form of participation demonstrated by all is important to the outcomes for all. To be effective, instructors should post the resulting agreements to the course Web site, for instance, and also refer to them throughout the term, such as noting when they are demonstrated or, perhaps, contradicted or ignored.

Conclusion

> *Students are not likely to gain intercultural competenc[e] by osmosis alone; they must be exposed in practices and understandings of the "other" and actively involved in an intercultural experience. That can be achieved through purposeful tasks through which they can develop the capacity to observe, to explore, to listen and to ask questions [Gesche and Makeham, 2008, p. 247].*

Engaging diversity in the classroom requires that instructors design relevant, substantive opportunities for students to explore multiple points of view and practice and refine communication skills in diverse contexts. This chapter has provided a foundation for and illustrations of how the principles of intercultural pedagogy may be implemented during the design phase. The next chapter turns to a discussion of the stage of implementation and facilitation.

Practicing a Pedagogy That Engages Diversity

ANY COURSE CAN ENGAGE STUDENTS IN INTERACTIONS that stimulate the cognitive and relational work that is fundamental to the development of intercultural competences. However, as any experienced instructor will observe, even the most careful course design is only the prologue to a messy classroom reality.

For example, you enter the classroom well prepared. As soon as you invite students into the discussion, a few of the regulars speak up, students who are confident expressing their opinions, comfortable extroverts who have educational histories of being affirmed for ready participation and rich contributions. A few others join in with slightly different perspectives. Then, a student who only occasionally speaks during discussion and who is visibly hesitant and anxious provides a radically different analysis of the reading. As this student is talking, you can see and feel the anxiety of some other students. As soon as the student is finished, other students immediately launch into what may be perceived as harsh dismissals or rebuttals to what was just articulated. Taken aback, you respond in ways that are perhaps more passive, hesitant, or silencing than you intend. You find yourself puzzling over how to better facilitate or structure dialogue toward your purposes the next time and wondering how to support students' ability to engage cognitive dissonance and multiple perspectives.

This scenario is not just reserved for novice instructors or disciplines that address overtly contentious topics. Every classroom has complex opportunities, acknowledged or not, to promote or thwart the contributions of students. Any course can engage students in interactions that stimulate the cognitive and relational work that is fundamental to the development of intercultural competence. Yet as we have argued throughout the monograph, the failure to utilize the opportunities present in our classrooms is detrimental to the goal of deepening our own and our students' capacity to listen and contribute in conversations that feature diverse ideas or communication styles. However, it is one thing to design a course based on the theory of intercultural development; it is another thing to be able to facilitate purposeful, substantive interactions in the midst of complex, unpredictable, and fluid dynamics in the classroom. Yet as Hurtado (2001) concluded from her research on climate and diversity, it is critical to consider how and whether our pedagogical practice promotes "the type of interaction necessary to create equal status conditions and, thus, learning in diverse environments" (p. 189). Therefore, this chapter shifts out of the course design stage to focus on a discussion of facilitative practices that support the development of intercultural skills in "real-time" learning environments with students present.

Applying Intercultural Pedagogical Principles to Classroom Facilitation

Drawing on the intercultural theory presented in earlier chapters, the following sections highlight specific pedagogical practices that are constructive for the development of intercultural learning outcomes. The selection of the practices that follow was guided by their solid grounding in both intercultural principles and research on teaching and learning. We illustrate each practice with excerpts from student learning reflections to emphasize how learning-centered perspectives can inform reflection and refinement of pedagogical practice. In order to model the balance between reflection and practical tools for teaching and learning, we also embed each suggested practice within a broader context that shapes the possibilities and constraints present in today's college classrooms.

Acknowledge Anxiety and Offer Support
Any classroom setting, but especially a diverse one, involves group interactions that are inherently anxiety producing (Gudykunst and Shapiro, 1996; Ickes, 1984). Despite the discomfort it provokes, disequilibrium is known to inspire

significant learning (Weinstein and Obear, 1992). A well-facilitated classroom can also offer students a safe context in which to develop productive ways of managing their anxiety by actively experimenting with new ways to deal with the unfamiliar. As we established in the third chapter, the goal is not to eliminate anxiety or discomfort, but to support students' capacity to manage them, as the ability to manage uncertainty or anxiety is crucial to intercultural learning.

Be Mindful of Different Thresholds of Anxiety. Gudykunst (2005) claimed that each person has a maximum and minimum threshold for uncertainty and anxiety. The maximum is defined as "the highest amount of uncertainty [one] can have and think [one] can predict strangers' behavior sufficiently to feel comfortable interacting with them" (Gudykunst, 2005, p. 286). That class events will sometimes elicit anxiety from both students and instructors is a given, and there are many occasions when our discomfort is warranted. When the anxiety passes a certain threshold, however, it begins to interfere with the learning process.

For example, this student identifies a language barrier as a significant source of anxiety in cooperative learning:

> *One moment when I felt really frustrated in class was within a group with two other girls. We were talking about a question [related to] the reading. I was trying to get across how I thought this question was logically answered in the text. They could not grasp my thoughts. Although there was a bit of a language barrier between us, it was as if they just dismissed my thought completely and moved on to their own beliefs. I felt misunderstood and unimportant to my other two group members.*

This student notes that the other two group members were multilingual and she spoke only English. She subsequently shuts down and does not make further attempts to be heard by or listen to her group.

Given the inevitability of such tension or anxiety in interactions across diversity, our job as instructors is to provide mechanisms to normalize the anxious response, but also to challenge and support students' ability to move beyond it or through it. In the preceding example, the instructor might respond by acknowledging the tension, reiterating that the voices of all group members are important, and gently encouraging the more outspoken students to make sure others feel heard before inserting their own opinions into the conversation.

Excessive anxiety can be activated in a variety of ways, but one of its most profound triggers concerns individual and group identity. Whether or not identity is the explicit focus of a discussion or activity, anxiety can be triggered by perceptions students bring into the classroom about their own and others' group membership. Anxiety can be especially at issue for students who do not represent the majority group in a classroom. They are more likely to fear negative consequences of classroom interactions, such as being discriminated against or negatively evaluated by members of other groups and those from their own group. All these fears are directly related to identity, and research literature highlights them as significant anxiety risks (Stephan and Stephan, 1985). When students perceive themselves to be in the "outgroup," they may often feel stereotyped or judged, regardless of whether they are part of a minority or majority group (Gonzales and others, 1983; Gudykunst, 2002; Ting-Toomey, 2005). When that occurs, anxiety becomes a significant barrier to learning.

Affirms Students' Self-Identity. Research suggests that an individual's anxiety can be decreased by the affirmation of their self-esteem and increased empathy that comes when they learn to introduce more nuance into their categorization of strangers (Gudykunst, 2005, p. 300). When students experience anxiety in the learning process, it is important for instructors to validate their identities as expressed in the classroom and to invite them to look deeper into the identities of others. Deardorff (2009b) argues that "the degree to which an individual feels secure in his or her identity" (p. 266) is a critical part of effectively engaging diverse perspectives and communicating effectively. Our role as instructors is to mediate the "tug of war" between comfort and frustration (Goodman, 2008).

An example of a classroom space that decreased anxiety by providing an opportunity for students to proactively assert their identities comes from a learning journal written by a student who noted that her family had immigrated to the United States and that she was the first in her family to go to college. She described herself as being shy, tending to prefer to listen to others, and often being the last to speak up in class. She experienced something of a turning point when required to present to the class on a biographical object and its significance:

> We had to write about a biographical object and to talk about it. During this time, not knowing everyone, I was really shy. . . . Many classes that I had before did not give us the chance to know one another. I think when students are able to interact and know more about one another, I believe it creates a better learning atmosphere. No one would feel left out. I was able to get to know my classmates better and they were able to get to know be better. Another reason why I chose this event was because I got to tell the class who I was. Many times people can judge me wrongly, and so by telling the class who I was really eliminates the stereotyping towards me. It showed them who I really was.

Activities such as this one help instructors to understand and affirm students' unique backgrounds, gain a sense of their possible anxiety thresholds, and scaffold activities that engage the range of identities within the classroom.

Model Tolerance for Ambiguity. If students are to learn how to tolerate ambiguity and manage their anxiety with the unfamiliar, they need the instructor to act as a constructive role model. Research by Weinstein and Obear (1992) shows that fear of experiencing intense emotions and losing control in the classroom is one of the top barriers faced by faculty in successfully engaging diversity in classrooms. Yet the level of anxiety in the classroom will increase exponentially if the instructor himself or herself appears uncomfortable with the content or student responses, and students will usually notice our anxiety even if not expressed.

Contrary to popular assumption, managing our own anxiety does not require that we always hide it behind a calm veneer. Experienced faculty know when their own or a student's emotional response begins to get in the way of the course. When that happens, it is helpful to pause the activity and notice the anxiety out loud. Weinstein and Obear (1992) point out that sometimes voicing our own ambivalence about stirring up feelings can be a good preventative practice in the classroom. Addressing anxiety directly in a way that communicates respect frees students to put a name to their own feelings, and removes the affective barrier that prevents genuine learning and engagement.

For example, racial identity, race relations, and racism are often an anxiety-producing topic in formal curricula across a broad range of humanities and social science courses. As discussed in the third chapter, racial tensions are also present in our classrooms due to the vastly different lived experiences of our students. Discussing the historic privileging of some populations and their differential access to systems of power can stir feelings of anxiety, uncertainty, and other emotional responses. In such cases, what often emerges in classrooms is a challenging and disorienting mix of emotions about race, ranging from guilt or depression to anger that the faculty member is pushing the class into material that is too difficult to deal with. Instructors may be inclined to try and avoid discussion and focus on presentation of the formal content in order to avoid conflict or unpredictability. Students may frustrate each other by debating differences between prejudice and racism and confusing their meanings as defined by scholars. At such times, the classroom can move rapidly from being placid to loud with competing emotions or, conversely, to silence as students and faculty retreat to safer and neater emotional places. These can be effective opportunities for faculty to share that they, too, wrestle with the anxiety, and to acknowledge that given the history of the United States, it is natural for persons to have vastly different experiences and interpretations. Conversations that name the anxiety present in the room, when authentic and given adequate time and space, can open expressions of trust and confidence that students can handle the dissonance productively. They also communicate to students that it is natural to feel discomfort when presented with material that challenges prior experiences, orientations, or social beliefs. For example, an instructor might say: "Let's take a time-out for a second: I'm not sure if you feel this as well, but discussing this topic is making me uncomfortable. Is anybody else feeling this as well? Why do you think we get uncomfortable when this topic comes up?" What can follow is a frank discussion in which the class is allowed to unpack the present anxiety and remove the affective barriers to learning by directly naming them.

Acknowledging the affective domain in the classroom counteracts the harmful perception that learning is exclusively an affair of the mind and engages powerful sources of student motivation. Students will stay up late in the night exploring issues that they feel strongly about, and they often decide to pursue career paths paved by affective motivations. A classroom climate where dissonance is expected, ambiguity is tolerated, and anxiety is respectfully acknowledged enables students to maintain a healthy curiosity in the course content as well as the diverse identities and perspectives of their classmates. How students view peers in class and the ease they feel in contributing, critiquing, and considering ideas with each other have direct implications for their level of engagement with diversity and their development of both cognitive and affective diversity competencies.

Disrupt Social Relations in the Classroom

As noted in earlier chapters, the mere presence of diversity in the classroom does not guarantee constructive interaction or skill development—without proper conditions it can, in fact, lead to the perpetuation of inequality and stereotype (Hurtado, 2001; Pettigrew and Tropp, 2006; Saenz, 2010). As Deardorff and Hunter (2006) observe, "too often, students remain segregated by their cultural backgrounds and institutions miss amazing opportunities to make the most of these resources in developing students' intercultural and global competencies" (p. 81). While this kind of segregation may occur broadly on college and university campuses, each classroom offers opportunities to productively and ethically interrupt segregation within classrooms so as to support students' substantive interactions with others (Arkoudis and others, 2010; Goodman, 2008; Hanson, 2010; Van Gyn, Schuerholz-Lehr, Caws, and Preece, 2009).

Respond to Triggers and Biased Comments. One specific question often asked by faculty with regard to promoting positive peer communication and relations in the classroom has to do with responding to biased comments made by students. In a paper devoted to such triggers in the classroom, Weinstein and Obear (1992) note that biased comments that touch on the identity of others, such as "I don't see race as an issue," "homosexuals are abnormal," or

"Jews aren't the only ones that suffered" (p. 45), often generate defensiveness on the part of the person or group being referenced, and they end in frustration or unproductive debates. If the instructor does not respond to these comments, targeted students feel threatened and unsupported. Simply remaining silent sends a message to those students who feel objectified or reduced by the comment. However, Weinstein and Obear (1992) point out that addressing them immediately in the moment can generate aggression or shut down discussion. Therefore, Weinstein and Obear (1992) advise a multipronged approach for dealing with such triggers. First, set a context and prepare by talking about them early on in the class; this should include establishing a way of handling them when they do arise. They suggest that instructors elicit examples of triggers from students at the outset of the class so that the concept is clear. Subsequently, when a trigger occurs, the student writes the phrase or comment and pastes it on the board or to the course Web site, so it can be analyzed and addressed. Weinstein and Obear suggest that suspending the discussion of the trigger enables some reflective distance to develop "between the person who gave the trigger and analysis of the trigger itself. The focus can then be on understanding the concept rather than dealing with the defenses of individuals" (p. 46).

Challenge Self-Grouping Habits. We were recently reminded of the importance of paying attention to obvious cues, such as who sits where, and whom they sit next to. For instance, at a recent college event related to our Common Read for first-year students, the guest lecturer noted to the 450 students present:

> It is interesting that you are asking me how to make a difference for refugee students in my community, thousands of miles away, and yet when I look around this auditorium, I can't help noticing where you all chose to sit. Look around. Who are you sitting next to? Who are you not sitting next to? There is a lot of diversity in this room. We are here to talk about working together across differences to support one another. But for the most part, all of you are sitting with people who look like you. How do you expect to do anything if you don't even get to know one another?

One of the essential principles for teaching and learning in multicultural contexts is the necessity to actively disrupt the status quo by creating salient groups in which members have an incentive and structure to work cooperatively toward a tangible common goal (Banks and others, 2001). Hurtado (2001) noted that, ". . . without attention to the structure of peer groups in diverse classrooms and to learning activities that promote interaction on an equal status basis, peer status can actually reproduce inequality and undermine the potential learning that can occur among diverse peers" (p. 190). When forming groups for collaborative learning activities, many instructors seek to support intercultural development outcomes by intentionally assembling groups in ways that will disrupt students' habits of self-grouping. Instructors should also be mindful of research that indicates students may feel more secure and comfortable if the group they are assigned to includes at least one other person whom they perceive as belonging to the same social group (Gudykunst, 2005). That said, it is important to keep in mind that not all forms of cultural and experiential diversity are visible, nor are they made public by students. Attention to both visible and invisible forms of diversity will enhance the design of purposeful collaborative activities and mechanisms for facilitating the development of effective group dynamics.

Facilitate Purposeful Small Groups. Ultimately, instructors are well served by investing time and attention in the design and implementation of group activities, and particularly in ensuring the intended learning and development outcomes are being achieved. One student's learning reflection on the first four weeks of class illustrates the gap that may emerge between thoughtful design and implementation. She was frustrated by the instructor's decision to form different groups in each class in order to promote more interactions across the large number of students. To facilitate that process, groups engaged in icebreaker activities. For this student, the rationale was both unclear and unachieved: "Forcing people to socialize just makes it more awkward and the students feel they are being forced. Real connections can't be made if we are constantly forced to change our seating." From this student's perspective, there was an absence of meaningful, relevant opportunities to interact and potentially form "real connections"; whereas, from the instructors' standpoint, it is likely the shifting of groups and icebreakers were intended to support interaction and connection. This example reinforces the importance of both structuring opportunities for frequent interaction and repeatedly assessing how groups are functioning.

Many instructors have found it helpful to assign students to the same peer group for the initial few weeks of the semester so that students can begin to feel confident among their peers, and mixing up the opportunities for broader interaction once the level of anxiety is somewhat decreased. Assessing the functioning of small groups is another crucial aspect of successful classroom management across time. When students are working in small groups during class, it is not sufficient for the instructor to assign the task and stay in the front of the room—checking in on students as they work in small groups allows the instructor to monitor what is happening and interrupt the activity when it is not functioning as intended. Many instructors have also found it useful to gather periodic written feedback from students on how the small-group work is helping or not helping their learning.

A particularly successful example of a staggered small-group experience comes from a recent public speaking and communications class. At the beginning of the semester, students were placed into groups of three. In these groups, they worked on small-group communication exercises that incorporated topics that were being discussed in their course. At one point, as they were discussing how different cultural groups form associations with certain behaviors as normal or abnormal and react accordingly, the groups were asked to come up with a norm-breaking activity. As a small group, they had to go to a public space and together break a social norm. Each member of the small group then had to reflect upon the experience. Together, the course content, group nature of activity, and subsequent required reflection enabled a deeper exploration of course concepts, while also providing a common experience that lowered their social inhibitions and helped them get to know one another.

Assign Collaborative Tasks. Research also suggests that relations between different groups of students in our classrooms will be more equal and positive if there is an explicitly collaborative dimension to learning activities or assignments (Hurtado, 2001; Wong, 2006). The positive interaction inherent in collaboration stems from shared goals and a visible alignment of interests: when one member of the group gains, so do the other members. It is important to make the benefits and outcomes of collaborative learning tangible and visible and to reinforce them in practice. During the initial phases of interaction in the classroom, collaboration may lead to considerable anxiety due to the close contact and coordination required. Overall, however, collaborative learning has demonstrated value in enhancing the academic achievement of students across racial and ethnic groups and in reducing prejudice. Social relations in the classroom can be restructured in positive ways as students practice and improve their interaction skills with students from different backgrounds (Hurtado, 2001; Slavin, 1995). Crossing of racial and cultural boundaries occurs more easily in "a supportive environment with structures that encourage investigation and reflection in conjunction with opportunities for meaningful, sustained, face-to-face interaction among people who are different from one another" (Wong, 2006, p. 1).

One example of how an instructor incorporated collaborative projects into the course comes from a civil engineering course for upper-level engineering students. The main focus of the course was transportation planning (that is, traffic flow principles, geometric and pavement design). The professor had recently worked on a project with several colleagues in India, and she developed several problem-based scenarios based on her own experiences working on this international collaborative project. She selected groups for the project based on previous knowledge of students' experiences (both with the course information and international context) and gave each group the same goal of developing an innovative solution to a specific planning problem. She asked each group to begin by discussing the strengths each member of the group brings in relation to the given scenario. Next, students were asked to consider additional information they may need to gather to more fully understand the transportation problem, such as technical data and local context, and to think about the most effective way to present the solution to coworkers in India. In this example, students all had a core base of knowledge from the course and previous coursework in the major. But they were given the task of working collaboratively on applying this knowledge in a unique context in a foreign country. Some groups sought information from friends who had grown up in

India; some even connected with students studying engineering at a local university in the area whose transportation issue they were trying to solve. At the end of the project, the instructor asked each member of the group to reflect upon what they learned about their group members, about the process of applying their knowledge in a unique context, and about themselves. Although this assignment involved higher stakes than other collaborative exercises described in this book, it allowed the instructor to incorporate students' diverse knowledge into the application of course content while at the same time facilitating productive understanding among diverse peers.

Model the Balance Between Suspending Judgment and Constructive Critique

In the second and third chapters, we argued that the ability to suspend judgment is a critical skill in relating to people of other cultures and backgrounds. Research suggests that it is not uncommon for students to enter college with a sincere but shallow conviction that everyone has the right to their own culture and opinion, underscored by an untested or passive-aggressive tolerance that does not amount to a mature suspension of judgment. While in college, many students pass through a stage described in the research literature as multiplicity (Perry, 1999), when they assume all cultures and perspectives to be equal without fully owning their own commitments or acknowledging the hard work involved in communicating or accomplishing goals in the presence of difference. We hear many of our students expressing a narrative common in our society that we term *happy diversity*, where everyone gets along and difference brings richness, not conflict or competing interests. For instance, in a learning reflection, one of our student shifts within the space of a few sentences from describing being "dismissed" and "misunderstood" by peers who were from a different cultural identity group than she to describing the class as "a community full of different ethnicities, backgrounds and beliefs . . . a large social group whose diversities can be incorporated into one big family."

The "performance" of a positive attitude toward diversity is well rehearsed and reiterated in schools and culture at large. This is one of the reasons why it takes time and multiple opportunities for individuals to reach a more mature stage in their development, where they can embrace their commitments and values, practice critical responses to their own and others' perspectives, and remain open to new information (King and Baxter Magolda, 2005).

In the past, some instructors may have considered suspending judgment as a major barrier in making room for intercultural competence in their classrooms. It is a common misconception that recognizing and inviting multiple perspectives precludes constructive critique, and that such an approach will make our courses less rigorous (Yershova, DeJeaghere, and Mestenhauser, 2000). Yet suspending judgment is in fact a prerequisite for critical thinking, since effective critique depends on a comprehensive understanding of a problem or issue within a context. Suggestive evidence that this is true comes up in case studies of student assessments of various types of classroom interaction (Lee, Williams, and Kilaberia, 2011). For instance, one student described how cooperative learning activities developed both her openness to diverse perspectives and her sense that she became more adept at engaging complex ideas in her writing:

> . . . getting the opportunity to work with people I usually would not work with . . . throughout the time in this class has opened my eyes to all different perspectives. . . . I have had to learn to be more open to other opinions, and more willing to express my thoughts. . . . I think having more than one opinion on something helps tons more when writing or explaining something later on. . . . Being able to write our thoughts about a specific subject, and have someone else break it down and revise it, helps me to write better. . . . I feel like three people's ideas are better than one person because we all see the issues differently.

Since many different courses assign peer review of assignments or papers, we will use it as an example to elaborate on how to incorporate constructive critique into intercultural classrooms. Peer review can be implemented in a traditional way that positions it as a one-way transaction: the reader performs peer review *for* the writer, who is the beneficiary if the review is helpful, or the victim in the case it is shallow. In situations where student writers have different writing styles or levels of awareness of the discourse conventions, peer review can reinforce discomfort between reviewers. In the absence of clear guidance and induction into peer review skills and outcomes by the instructor, it is not unusual for students to focus on mechanical elements of grammar, for instance, and to elide altogether issues of substance, perspective, or interpretation because they do not want to "criticize."

There are multiple levels of potential benefits, however, when peer review is structured and implemented as a mutually beneficial and cooperative interaction. Instructors can make clear to all students the value of critically engaging a piece of in-process writing through the act of close reading, paying attention to how it is composed, noticing and articulating which elements are effective and where attention is needed. We can do that by communicating to students that completing a peer review is not only for the writer of the text reviewed but for the peer reviewer, who can incorporate the fruits of this reflection on someone else's text-in-process when they return to their own. Modeling for students how to probe a piece of writing is beneficial to many of the outcomes related to intercultural competence if students can see firsthand how to pose questions about the logic, interpretations, or substantiation of claims in a piece of writing in ways that do not target the writing but critically engage it.

Additionally, many students are uncomfortable providing peer review because they do not perceive that they are "experts" in the subject matter or in writing generally. Guiding students in how to provide effective review, as well as in what is to be gained from it by all participants, can help to build confidence in their ability to participate effectively by taking the spotlight off of their "performance" as a reviewer and creating an understanding that peer review is truly a cooperative endeavor that, when done well, will facilitate positive outcomes for all participants. This excerpt provides an illustration of how effectively facilitated peer review can support both writing skills and outcomes related to intercultural competence. The student cited above notes his initial interpretation of encountering difference, which he identifies simultaneously in cultural background and writing style: "working with a classmate . . . from a very different cultural background than me was a definite learning experience. The biggest struggle I had was when it came to language because she had a very different writing style than I was used to so it took me some time to be able to grasp what it was that she was trying to say."

His reflection illustrates an ability to suspend judgment of his awareness of the difference and to remain open to the potential benefits of interaction. He concludes with the observation that, ultimately, "working and getting to know people who have very different cultural backgrounds . . . really helped me develop as a writer."

We can also model the balance of developing critical thinking skills and suspending judgment by seeking to evaluate the claims or perspectives heard in class only when they have been thoroughly observed and understood. For instance, before providing critique, an instructor might say, "Let me see if I understood you correctly. So you're saying that . . ." Sometimes, hearing their own statement repeated back in different words will prompt the student to clarify a potential misunderstanding or recognize why it might raise objections. In any case, verifying comprehension before providing a critique will model a mature suspension of judgment to the class.

The final point on the place of critique in classrooms that aim to develop intercultural outcomes is the recognition that critique must not elicit shame. Shame has devastating effects on motivation and academic learning (Turner and Schallert, 2001). When students are shamed, they come up against affective barriers to learning even more disruptive than those built up by anxiety. Educational psychologists claim that shame is a "master emotion" (Goldberg, 1991) in that "no other emotion plays such a central role in affective, cognitive, motivational, and behavioral experiences" (Turner and Schallert, 2001, p. 320). Lewis (1992) claimed that shame acts as an authoritative "interrupt signal" that lets the individual know that their actions have failed, and shuts down or disrupts engagement in these actions. When students experience shame while participating in positive activities such as collaborative work or dialogue across diversity, they internalize the message that these actions have failed, and they are less likely to attempt them again. Instructors can avoid shaming by making a point to distinguish between a behavior or belief and the person (Goodman, 1995), and validating identity while evaluating statements or behaviors. When providing such validating critique, an instructor might say, "I see what you mean, and many very intelligent people reach a similar conclusion. How would it affect your opinion if you learned that . . ." or "How do you think you would see this problem differently if you were a [member of a different social group]?" Validating the person and focusing on the issue minimizes defensive barriers and opens up a space where students feel safe to put themselves in the shoes of others and explore new ideas.

Facilitate Conditions to Support Inclusive Dialogue

Our role as instructors is to support and structure an environment where students can develop more mindful behaviors. One of the main ways to facilitate students' development is to create interactions in which students are heard, feel comfortable, and trust one another to explore and engage across cultures and various disciplinary content arenas.

Manage the Stages of Interaction. It is especially helpful to incorporate activities where, in the first stage, students cannot express evaluative judgments about the other person's views—the emphasis is on listening and interpreting. Keeping students in the same groups for several similar exercises within a short space of interactive class time helps them to practice listening and interpretive skills with a stranger whose language, perspectives, and interpretations they can observe several times. This process provides space for skill development as students recognize that their views and interpretations are not necessarily those of others, and that there can be value in actively listening to an alternative perspective and being accountable to represent it accurately without first interjecting a dissonant point of view. The following student reflection illustrates the interpersonal group process when people are given the time to get to know each other before accomplishing concrete tasks:

> When we first sat down next to each other, we did not start talking until we were instructed to. After receiving the instructions to talk to each other, we all started making small talk about what classes we were taking and where we were from. I think we were all just trying to feel each other out to see if we would work well with each other. Although I thought it would be a really awkward situation, we all started laughing with each other once our comfort levels were established. I realized that maybe I could be friends with these two girls and it would not just have to be a project where three random people were put in a group and were forced to work with

each other. We all discovered that we had the same goal of doing
well in the class and once this was established . . . we realized that
working together might not be half bad.

Kumagai and Lypson (2009) also suggest that effective group discussions require instructors to facilitate but not preside over the conversation. When students connect and engage in dialogue with each other, the classroom gains a sense of community that is not present when all main avenues of communication lead back to the instructor. Such sense of community has been demonstrated to have significant educational benefits. McKinney, McKinney, Franiuk, and Schweitzer (2006), for instance, found that "the sense of community has shown to relate not only to students' perception of their performance and their satisfaction with the course but also the measure of their actual performance" (p. 283).

Welcome Different Styles of Communication. For all students to engage in genuine dialogue, the facilitator must attend to the communication styles of diverse groups. For instance, introverts and students from some cultural backgrounds are acculturated to the need to allow silence before speaking. Goodman (2008) suggests that these students will benefit from incorporating intentional periods of silence into every class. Different communication styles will also be normalized for students if at least some class activities require everyone to think for a brief period of time before responding or providing answers. Margaret Montoya, a professor at the University of New Mexico, introduces silence in her classroom in the following way:

I explain that some students are prepared to answer quite rapidly
while others are slower in preparing a response. Despite the con-
ventional wisdom that overvalues quickness, I announce that I will
wait for those who do not think aloud and who need more time to
collect their thoughts before speaking. My purpose is to give those
who need more time the opportunity to pause and process their
thoughts without having to fear that they will be interrupted by
those who are quicker to speak (the "crowders"). I want to help the
students hear each others [sic] silences and defeat the tendency to

reach negative conclusions about pauses and hesitancy [Montoya, 2000, pp. 297–298].

By the same token, when students are engaged in large-group discussion, students from some groups will be more likely to provide ready answers or raise their hands to volunteer information. If the instructor selects only volunteers, the voices of those representing different communication patterns are likely to be excluded. A practical solution that works well for some instructors is to invite students to self-score on the participation grade based on the idea that extroverts may need to focus on listening, while introverts need to focus on speaking in class. Around midsemester, each student reflects on his or her own performance, and makes suggestions for earning the remaining participation points in the coming weeks. Students are then graded based on their own goals selected at the midterm point, such as: I need to listen more, I need to speak up more, etc.[2]

Conclusion

This chapter has presented pedagogical practices and reflective practices that support faculty's ability to facilitate *engaged* diversity in their classes. Developing intercultural competence rests on knowledge acquisition in conjunction with building the capacity to implement that knowledge across diverse contexts; in other words, it requires *knowing about* and *knowing about how to do*. Developing the capacity to *do* requires multiple and longitudinal opportunities to acquire knowledge, as well as to apply and refine it.

Barker and Crichton (2010) describe the potential of classrooms to serve as authentic sites of intercultural interactions, or engaging diversity, concepts that refer to, "opportunities provided in courses and taken by students and instructors to participate in and to thereby negotiate and develop new cultural understandings of themselves and others" (Barker and Crichton, 2010, p. 31). In order to utilize these opportunities, faculty need to recognize them, design pedagogy to realize them, and facilitate students' learning and development while they are taking place.

As we have established throughout this monograph, developing intercultural pedagogy is a continuous, interactive process that takes place over time.

Those who have attended workshops related to teaching development, whether on implementing learning technologies or incorporating active learning, may be familiar with the experience of being exposed to new knowledge and possibilities. Handouts and notes present extensive content, and one often leaves with a sense of eagerness to implement some new tools. Yet, given that it is unlikely that the localized factors and nuances of one's classroom will be accounted for in a workshop, participants often express feeling challenged, after attending a workshop, to find the time, support, and space needed *to reflect* on how to integrate and implement new ideas or tools into their specific teaching contexts. The same is likely to be true for the readers of this monograph. Resources such as this book are just the beginning as far as developing intercultural pedagogy—knowledge, reflection, experimentation, and interaction with others are all critical to our ability to implement the new tools. Instructors need authentic contexts in which to develop effective intercultural pedagogy and to reflect on our practice with the goal of refinement. Similarly, students need authentic sites of intercultural interaction and opportunity to practice, reflect, and refine intercultural skills, attitudes, and behaviors. Instructors reading this monograph will need to find time, space, and support (perhaps from colleagues or professional communities) to *develop* effective intercultural pedagogy that is informed by and responsive to authentic contexts of practice, and to continuously assess practice with the goal of refinement.

Summary: Conclusions and Recommendations

THE WRITING OF THIS MONOGRAPH EMERGED from a passion for teaching rooted in a deep belief that students bring great value to classrooms. This value is realized and expanded through the active engagement of their diversity with others. When such diversity is honored and utilized productively by faculty, student interactions can produce enhanced exploration of course content, deeper intellectual inquiry, and the development of intercultural communication skills.

The capacity to communicate effectively across human difference is vital to the success of this nation, which is already among the most culturally diverse on earth. There is an established need for graduates who can work collaboratively and communicate effectively with diverse colleagues, neighbors, and community members. An interculturally competent individual has developed the ability to respectfully hear, communicate within, utilize, and appreciate human difference in all of its forms—all of which hold powerful capacity to unify and strengthen a multicultural society such as ours.

It is entirely consistent with the historic meaning and contemporary need of colleges and universities to engage all students and facilitate their interaction as one way of developing competencies relevant to their common benefit and that of society at large. Indeed, the historic meaning of "university" refers to "the totality of a group"—a group that could be unified for common benefit (Haskins, 1957, p. 9). The U.S. Supreme Court underscored this point in past decisions holding that diversity in classrooms is of such high value that race can be considered as one factor in collegiate admissions. We recognize that there are practitioners who are "on the ground" with an immediate need for theory-based models that are grounded in the realities of classroom contexts and realities. We trust that the scholarship included within this monograph provide a pragmatic foundation from which faculty can mindfully prepare for and act within their classroom settings.

We stated throughout this monograph that the development of intercultural competence can occur within classrooms and across disciplines whether in the humanities, social sciences, or in STEM fields. As faculty, we have the ability to facilitate such competence development when mindful of the purposes and actions that are necessary to guide students into interactions that are inclusive of their respective differences and productively disrupt patterns of non-engagement or the mindless acceptance or rejection of difference. Further, we have the ability to interrupt historically privileged modes of inquiry and interpretation and open our classrooms to the alternative forms of inquiry and meaning-making that diverse students bring. While this can take different forms within different disciplines, space can be provided in any classroom for students to engage interculturally in the exploration of new questions and concepts. If done intentionally, this process can support students' capacity development of skills, knowledge, and behaviors that enable effective and reciprocal interaction and communication. As the students' reflections throughout this monograph help demonstrate, classrooms can be designed so as to serve as wonderfully dynamic places where intellectual and social energy emerges from respectful intercultural interactions united in a quest to understand the nuances of an academic discipline or field.

The substantial body of published research reviewed in this monograph supports our contention that each time we enter a classroom, we have the power to model, develop, and influence intercultural communication skills while simultaneously conveying important disciplinary content. When their lived experience and cultural perspectives are viewed as assets, students can be invited into intellectual engagements that demonstrate the power and relevance of their individual and collective diversity. Faculty have great ability to communicate repeatedly to students that they bring valued, relevant knowledge to the classroom by stating it in their syllabi, designing and selecting course materials in a manner that intentionally invite intercultural communication. Providing time for facilitated, purposeful interactions honors and supports the intentional engagement of diversity.

As we conclude our review of the research that connects theory with classroom practice, we are aware that more research and collaboration are needed to describe more fully how to engage diversity and develop intercultural communication competencies in all disciplines and fields. While excellent work does exist in describing this in a variety of fields such as medical training, more is needed. This monograph references studies and practices in STEM fields that show the possibilities for intercultural communication development available within disciplines that are very different from our own. The *how* of our work—the ways in which we engage students and facilitate their interactions with each other—need not be unnecessarily limited by the *what* of our disciplinary content or their differences. We hope that faculty outside of our own particular disciplinary backgrounds and fields will invest in the meaningful preparation, design, and deployment of time and resources that engage students in intercultural competence development and will then further share how such interactions affect the query and dynamics of their classes.

Further, in addition to faculty commitment to classroom-based practices and applicable research, we do not underestimate the fundamental responsibility and impact of institutional support for engaging diversity. From providing ongoing development for faculty to ensuring admissions and graduation criteria that enact the priority of diversity and intercultural competence, institutions serve critical roles. Just as we have described the importance of an alignment between environment, pedagogy, and instructional practice in classes that support engaging diversity, it is critical for institutions to work on authentic and material alignments between institutional rhetoric, resource allocation, hiring and promotion practices, and curriculum in ways that push from espousing to enacting the value of diversity, and do not delimit its scope or impact. Institutional neglect in valuing diversity can have serious consequences well beyond the classroom in contemporary and future policy environments.

The U.S. Supreme Court will soon hear a case involving the University of Texas in which it is questioned how diversity is achieved on college and university campuses that receive public funding. This case, *Fisher v. University of Texas at Austin* (2011), once again places before the Supreme Court the issue of whether the admissions processes utilized by public colleges and universities can take race into account when making admissions decisions. It is probable then that the value of human diversity on college campuses will be revisited and fiercely debated. As previously noted, while the Court has historically recognized the value of a diverse student body to classroom interactions (*Regents of the University of California v. Bakke*, 1978; *Gratz v. Bollinger*, 2003; and *Grutter v. Bollinger*, 2003), such value should be expressed more fully and forcefully from within higher education. Past cases were aided by well-informed "friend of the Court" briefs that used experience-based research within colleges and universities to demonstrate the remarkable value that diverse students bring to campuses and classrooms when there is a commitment to and enactment of a culture of inclusive excellence.

We hope that additional higher education classroom-focused research from a broad array of disciplines and fields will further strengthen the evidence of how completely intercultural interactions and competencies among faculty and students contribute to learning and skill development and also this nation's well-being. Such well-being extends far beyond the respective concerns of employers who want skilled and collaborative workers or of collegiate officers who are weighing the legality of their admissions methodologies. It is a well-being rooted in the capacity of persons to interact for common benefit and development. Once again, we are reminded of Deardorff's (2009b) comment that, "in the end, intercultural competence is about our relationships with each other and, ultimately, our very survival as the human race, as we work together to address the global challenges that confront us" (p. 269).

Notes

1. A Research-1 institution is an institution with high research activity and over 50 programs awarding doctoral degrees each year.
2. We thank an anonymous reviewer for offering this suggestion.

References

Adler, P. S. (1972). Culture shock and the cross-cultural learning experience. In D. S. Hoopes (Ed.), *Readings in intercultural communications* (Vol. 2, pp. 6–21). Pittsburgh, PA: Regional Council on International Education.

Alger, J. R., and others. (2000). *Does diversity make a difference? Three research studies on diversity in college classrooms.* Washington, DC: American Council on Education.

Allport, W. (1954). *The nature of prejudice.* Reading, MA: Addison-Wesley.

Anderson, J. (2008). *Driving change through diversity and globalization: Transformative leadership in the academy.* Sterling, VA: Stylus.

Antonio, A. L. (2000). Developing leadership skills for diversity: The role of interracial interaction. Paper presented at the Annual American Educational Research Association in New Orleans, LA.

Antonio, A. L. (2004). The influence of friendship groups on intellectual self-confidence and educational aspirations in college. *Journal of Higher Education, 75*(4), 446–472.

Arasaratnam, L. A., and Doerfel, M. L. (2005). Intercultural communication competence: Identifying key components from multicultural perspectives. *International Journal of Intercultural Relations, 29*(2), 137–163.

Arkoudis, S., and others. (2010). *Finding common ground: Enhancing interaction between domestic and international students.* Melbourne: Australian Learning and Teaching Council.

Association of American Colleges and Universities (AAC&U). (2002). *Greater expectations: A new vision of learning as a nation goes to college.* Washington, DC: Association of American Colleges and Universities.

Association of American Colleges and Universities (AAC&U). (2005). *Making excellence inclusive series.* Washington, DC: Association of American Colleges and Universities.

Association of American Colleges and Universities (AAC&U). (2007). *College learning for a new global century.* Washington, DC: Association of American Colleges and Universities.

Association of American Colleges and Universities (AAC&U). (2010). *Raising the bar: Employers' views on college learning in the wake of the economic downturn.* Washington, DC: Association of American Colleges and Universities.

Banks, J. (1993). The canon debate, knowledge construction, and multicultural education. *Educational Researcher 22*, 4–14.

Banks, J. A., and others. (2001). Diversity within unity: Essential principles for teaching and learning in a multicultural society. *Phi Delta Kappa*, pp. 196–203.

Banks, J. A., and McGee, C. A. (1995). *Handbook of research on multicultural education*. Stanford, CA: Jossey-Bass.

Barker, S., and Crichton, J. (2008). Assessing and evaluating intercultural teaching and learning: An information management case study. *Journal of International Education in Business, 1*(1), 29–42.

Batson, C. D., Lishner, D. A., Cook, J., and Sawyer, S. (2005). Similarity and nurturance: Two possible sources of empathy for strangers. *Basic and Applied Social Psychology, 27*(1), 15–25.

Bennett, D. L., and Bennett, J. M. (2004). *Handbook of intercultural training*. Thousand Oaks, CA: Sage.

Bennett J. M., and Salonen, R. (2007). Intercultural communication and the new American campus. *Change, 39*(2), 46–50.

Bennett, M. J. (1993). Towards ethnorelativism: A development model of intercultural sensitivity. In R. Michael Paige (Ed.), *Education for the intercultural experience* (pp. 21–71). Yarmouth, ME: Intercultural Press.

Bok, D. (2006). *Our underachieving colleges: A candid look at how much students learn and why they should be learning more*. Princeton, NJ: Princeton University Press.

Boler M. (1999). *Feeling power: Emotions and education*. New York: Routledge.

Bowman, N. A. (2010a). Assessing learning and development among diverse college students. *New Directions for Institutional Research, 145*, 53–71. doi:10.1002/ir.322

Bowman, N. A. (2010b). College diversity experiences and cognitive development: A meta-analysis. *Review of Educational Research, 80*(1), 4–33. doi:10.3102/0034654309352495

Brown-Jeffy, S., and Cooper, J. E. (2011). Toward a conceptual framework of culturally relevant pedagogy: An overview of the conceptual and theoretical literature. *Teacher Education Quarterly 38*(1), 65–84.

Bruffee, K. A. (1999). *Collaborative learning: Higher education, interdependence, and the authority of knowledge*. Baltimore: Johns Hopkins University Press.

Byram, M. (1997). *Teaching and assessing intercultural communicative competence*. Philadelphia: Multilingual Matters.

Chang, M. J., Chang, J. C., and Ledesma, M. C. (2005). Beyond magical thinking: Doing the real work of diversifying our institutions. *About Campus, 10*(2), 9–16.

Chávez, A. F. (2011). Toward a multicultural ecology of teaching and learning: A critical review of theory and research. *Journal on Excellence in College Teaching, 21*(4), 26.

Chávez, A. F., Guido-DiBrito, F., and Mallory, S. L. (2003). Learning to value the "other": A framework of individual diversity development. *Journal of College Student Development, 44*(4), 453–469.

Christensen, L. (1989). Writing the word and the world. *English Journal*, pp. 14–18.

Clayton-Pedersen, A. R., O'Neill, N., and Musil, C. M. (2009). *Making excellence inclusive: A framework for embedding diversity and inclusion into college and universities' academic excellence mission*. Washington, DC: Association of American Colleges and Universities.

Clifford, J. (1991). The subject in discourse. In P. Harkin and J. Schilb (Eds.), *Contending with words* (pp. 38–51). New York: Modern Language Association.

Cupach, W., and Imahori, T. T. (1993). Identity management theory: Communication competence in intercultural episodes and relationships. In R. L. Wiseman and J. Koester (Eds.), *Intercultural communication competence* (Vol. 16). Newbury Park, CA: Sage.

Danowitz, M. A., and Tuitt, F. (2011). Enacting inclusivity through engaged pedagogy: A higher education perspective. *Equity and Excellence in Education*, *44*(1), 40–56. doi:10.1080/10665684.2011.539474

Day, P., and others. (2004). *Learning reconsidered: A campus-wide focus on the student experience*. Washington, DC: The National Association of Student Personnel Administrators and The American College Personnel Association.

Deardorff, D. K. (2004). *The identification and assessment of intercultural competence as a student outcome of internationalization at institutions of higher education in the United States* (Unpublished doctoral dissertation). North Carolina State University, Raleigh, NC.

Deardorff, D. K. (2006). Identification and assessment of intercultural competence as a student outcome of internationalization. *Journal of Studies in International Education*, *10*(3), 241–266.

Deardorff, D. K. (2009a). Preface. In D. K Deardorff (Ed.), *The Sage handbook of intercultural competence* (pp. xi–1). Thousand Oaks, CA: Sage.

Deardorff, D. K. (2009b). Synthesizing conceptualizations of intercultural competence: A summary and emerging themes. In D. K Deardorff (Ed.), *The Sage handbook of intercultural competence* (pp. 264–269). Thousand Oaks, CA: Sage.

Deardorff, D. K., and Hunter, W. (2006). Educating global-ready graduates. *International Educator*, *15*(3), 72–83.

Dehert, K., and Lagos, A. (Directors). (2003). *Underground* [Short film]. Los Angeles: Smashcut Films.

Denson, N. (2009). Do curricular and cocurricular diversity activities influence racial bias? A meta-analysis. *Review of Educational Research*, *79*(20), 805–838.

Denson, N., and Chang, M. J. (2009). Racial diversity matters: The impact of diversity-related student engagement and institutional context. *American Educational Research Journal*, *46*(2), 322.

Dewey, J. (1915). *The school and society: Being three lectures by John Dewey, supplemented by a statement of the university elementary school*. Chicago: University of Chicago Press, 1899; London: P. S. King, 1900; revised and enlarged edition, Chicago: University of Chicago Press, 1915; Cambridge: Cambridge University Press, 1915.

Dey, E. L., and others. (2010). *Engaging diverse viewpoints: What is the campus climate for perspective-taking?* Washington, DC: American Association of Colleges and Universities.

Dobbert, M. (1998). The impossibility of internationalizing students by adding materials to courses. In J. A. Mestenhauser and B. J. Ellingboe (Eds.), *Reforming the higher education curriculum: Internationalizing the campus* (pp. 53–68). Phoenix: Oryx Press.

Eisenchlas, S., and Trevaskes, S. (2007). Developing intercultural communication skills through intergroup interaction. *Intercultural Education, 18*(5), 413–425.

Ellsworth, E. (1989). Why doesn't this feel empowering? Working through the repressive myths of critical pedagogy. *Harvard Educational Review, 59*(3), 297–324.

Equality Challenge Unit. (2010). *Internationalisation and equality and diversity in higher education: Emerging identities.* London: Equality Challenge Unit. Retrieved February 15, 2012, from http://www.ecu.ac.uk/publications/files/joining-up-agendas-senior-management-briefing.pdf/view.

Equality Challenge Unit. (2011). *Joining up agendas: Internationalisation and equality and diversity in higher education.* London: Equality Challenge Unit. Retrieved February 15, 2012, from http://www.ecu.ac.uk/publications/internationalising-equality-equalising.

Fisher v. University of Texas at Austin, 631 F.3d 213 (5th Cir. 2011).

Gair, M., and Mullins, G. (2001). Hiding in plain sight. In E. Margolis (Ed.), *The hidden curriculum in higher education* (pp. 21–42). New York: Routledge.

Gallagher, C., and Lee. A. (2008). *Teaching writing that matters.* New York: Scholastic Press; Theory into Practice Series.

Gay, G. (2002). Preparing for culturally responsive teaching. *Journal of Teacher Education, 53*(2), 106–116.

Gesche, A., and Makeham, P. (2008). Creating conditions for intercultural and international learning and teaching. In M. Hellstén and A. M. Reid (Eds.), *Researching international pedagogies: Sustainable practice for teaching and learning in higher education* (pp. 241–258). New York: Springer.

Goldberg, C. (1991). *Understanding shame.* Lanham, MD: Aronson.

Gonzales, M. H., and others. (1983). Interactional approach to interpersonal attraction. *Journal of Personality and Social Psychology, 44*, 1192–1197.

Goodman, C. C. (2008). Retaining diversity in the classroom: Strategies for maximizing the benefits that flow from a diverse student body. *Pepperdine Law Review, 35*(3), 663–704.

Goodman, D. J. (1995). Difficult dialogues: Enhancing discussions about diversity. *College Teaching, 43*(2), 47–52.

Gore, J. (1993). *The struggle for pedagogies: Critical and feminist discourses as regimes of truth.* New York: Routledge.

Gottfredson, N. C., and others. (2008). Does diversity at undergraduate institutions influence student outcomes? *Journal of Diversity in Higher Education, 1*(2), 80–94.

Grandin, J. M., and Hedderich, N. (2009). Intercultural competence in engineering: Global competence for engineers. In D. Deardorff (Ed.), *Sage handbook on intercultural competence* (pp. 362–373). Thousand Oaks, CA: Sage.

Gratz v. Bollinger, 539 U.S. 244 (2003).

Green, M. F., and Shoenberg, R. (2006). *Where faculty live: Internationalizing the disciplines.* Washington, DC: American Council on Education.

Grutter v. Bollinger, 539 U.S. 306 (2003).

Gudykunst, W. B. (1993). Toward a theory of effective interpersonal and intergroup communication: An anxiety/uncertainty management (AUM) perspective. In R. L. Wiseman and J. Koester (Eds.), *Intercultural communication theory* (pp. 33–71). Newbury Park, CA: Sage.

Gudykunst, W. B. (1998). Applying the anxiety/uncertainty management (AUM) theory to intercultural adjustment training. *International Journal of Intercultural Relations, 22*(2), 227–250.

Gudykunst, W. B. (2002). Issues in cross-cultural communication research. In W. B. Gudykunst and B. Mody (Eds.), *Handbook of international and intercultural communication* (2nd ed., pp. 165–179). Thousand Oaks, CA: Sage.

Gudykunst, W. B. (2005). An anxiety/uncertainty management (AUM) theory of effective communication: Making the mesh of the net finer. In W. B. Gudykunst (Ed.), *Theorizing about intercultural communication* (pp. 281–349). Thousand Oaks, CA: Sage.

Gudykunst, W. B., and Shapiro, R. (1996). Communication in everyday interpersonal and intergroup encounters. *International Journal of Intercultural Relations, 20*, 19–45.

Gurin, P., Dey, E. L., Hurtado, S., and Gurin, G. (2002). Diversity and higher education: Theory and impact on educational outcomes. *Harvard Educational Review, 72*(3), 330–367.

Gurin, P., and Nagda, B.R.A. (2006). Getting to the what, how, and why of diversity on campus. *Educational Researcher, 35*(1), 20.

Gurin, P., Nagda, B.R.A., and Lopez, G. E. (2004). The benefits of diversity in education for democratic citizenship. *Journal of Social Issues, 60*(1), 17–34. doi: 10.1111/j.0022-4537.2004.00097.x

Hanson, L. (2010). Global citizenship, global health, and the internationalization of curriculum: A study of transformative potential. *Journal of Studies in International Education, 14*(1), 70–88.

Harper, S. R., and Antonio, A. L. (2008). Not by accident: Intentionality in diversity, learning, and engagement. In S. R. Harper (Ed.), *Creating inclusive campus environments for cross-cultural learning and student engagement* (pp. 1–18). Washington, DC: National Association of Student Personnel Administrators.

Harper, S. R., and Hurtado, S. (2007). Nine themes in campus racial climates and implications for institutional transformation. *New Directions for Student Services, 120*, 7–24. San Francisco: Jossey-Bass.

Harper, S. R., and Quaye, S. J. (2009). Beyond sameness, with engagement and outcomes for all: An introduction. In S. R. Harper and S. J. Quaye (Eds.), *Student engagement in higher education: Theoretical perspectives and practical approaches for diverse populations* (pp. 1–12). New York: Routledge.

Hartley, C. C., and Petrucci, C. J. (2004). Practicing culturally competent therapeutic jurisprudence: A collaboration between social work and law. *Journal of Law & Policy, 14*, 133–182.

Haskins, C. H. (1957). *The rise of universities*. Ithaca, NY: Cornell University Press.

Herrington, A., and Curtis, M. (2000). *Persons in process: Four stories of writing and personal development in college*. Urbana, IL: National Council of Teachers of English; Refiguring English Studies Series.

Hoffman, D. M. (2004). Internationalisation at home from the inside: Non-native faculty and transformation. *Journal of Studies in International Education, 7*, 77–93.

Hoskins, J. (1998). *The play of time: Kodi perspectives on calendars, exchange and history.* Berkeley: University of California Press.

Hu, S., and Kuh, G. D. (2003). Diversity experiences and college student learning and personal development. *Journal of College Student Development, 44*(3), 320–334.

Hurtado, S. (2001). Linking diversity and educational purpose: How diversity affects the classroom environment and student development. In G. Orfield (Ed.), *Diversity challenged: Evidence on the impact of affirmative action* (pp. 187–203). Cambridge, MA: Harvard Education Publishing Group.

Hurtado, S. (2005). The next generation of diversity and intergroup relations research. *Journal of Social Issues, 61*(3), 595–610.

Ickes, W. (1984). Compositions in black and white: Determinants of interaction in interracial dyads. *Journal of Personality and Social Psychology, 47,* 330–341.

Johnson, D. W., Johnson, R. T., and Smith, K. A. (1998). *Active learning: Cooperation in the college classroom.* Edina, MN: Interaction.

Johnson, K., and Inoue, Y. (2003). Diversity and multicultural pedagogy: An analysis of attitudes and practices within an American Pacific Island university. *Journal of Research in International Education 2*(3), 251–276. doi: 10.1177/1475240903002003001

Kegan, R. (1994). *In over our heads: The mental demands of modern life.* Cambridge, MA: Harvard University Press.

Kezar, A., Glenn, W., Lester, J., and Nakamoto, J. (2008). Examining organizational contextual features that affect implementation of equity initiatives. *Journal of Higher Education, 70*(2), 125–159.

Khaja, K., and others. (2011). Multicultural teaching: Barriers and recommendations. *Journal on Excellence in College Teaching, 21*(4), 5–28.

Kim, Y. Y. (2005). Association and dissociation: A contextual theory of interethnic communication. In W. B. Gudykunst (Ed.), *Theorizing about intercultural communication* (pp. 323–349). Thousand Oaks, CA: Sage.

Kim, Y. Y. (2009). The identity factor in intercultural competence. In D. K. Deardorff (Ed.), *The Sage handbook of intercultural competence* (pp. 53–65). Thousand Oaks, CA: Sage.

King, A. (2002). Structuring peer interaction to promote high-level cognitive processing. *Theory Into Practice, 41,* 33–39.

King, A. (2008). Structuring peer interaction to promote higher-order thinking and complex learning in cooperating groups. In R. M. Gillies, A. F. Ashman, J. Terwel, (Eds.), *The teacher's role in implementing cooperative learning in the classroom* (Vol. 8, pp. 73–91). New York: Springer.

King, P., and Howard-Hamilton, M. (2003). An assessment of multicultural competence. *Journal of Student Affairs Research and Practice, 40*(2). doi:10.2202/1949-6605.1226

King, P. M., and Baxter Magolda, M. B. (2005). A developmental model of intercultural maturity. *Journal of College Student Development, 46*(6), 571–592. doi: 10.1353/csd .2005.0061

Kolb, D. A. (1984). *Experiential learning: Experience as the source of learning and development.* Englewood Cliffs, NJ: Prentice-Hall.

Konrath, S. H., O'Brien, E. H., and Hsing, C. (2011). Changes in dispositional empathy in American college students over time: A meta-analysis. *Personality and Social Psychology Review*, *15*(2), 180.

Krutky, J. (2008). Intercultural competency: Preparing students to be global citizens. *Effective Practices for Academic Leaders*, *3*(1), 1–15.

Kuh, G. D., and others. (2007). Piecing together the student success puzzle: research, propositions, and recommendations. *ASHE Higher Education Report*, *32*(5). San Francisco: Jossey-Bass.

Kumagai, A. K., and Lypson, M. L. (2009). Beyond cultural competence: Critical consciousness, social justice, and multicultural education. *Academic Medicine*, *84*(6), 782.

Kuszewski, A. (n.d.). The educational value of creative disobedience. Guest blog, Scientific American Blog Network. Retrieved August 30, 2011, from http://blogs.scientificamerican .com/guest-blog/2011/07/07/the-educational-value-of-creative-disobedience/.

Ladson-Billings, G. (1995a). Toward a theory of culturally relevant pedagogy. *American Educational Research Journal*, *32*(3), 465–491. doi:10.2307/1163320

Ladson-Billings, G. (1995b). But that's just good teaching! The case for culturally relevant pedagogy. *Theory Into Practice*, *34*(3), 159–165.

Ladson-Billings, G. (1999). Preparing teachers for diverse student populations: A critical race theory perspective. *Review of Research in Education 24*, 211–247.

Langer, E. J. (1989). *Mindfulness*. New York: Addison-Wesley.

Langer, E. J. (1997). *The power of mindful learning*. New York: Addison-Wesley.

Langer, E. J., and Moldoveanu, M. (2000). The construct of mindfulness. *Journal of Social Issues*, *56*(1), 1–9.

Lee, A. (2001). *Composing critical pedagogies: Teaching writing as revision*. Urbana, IL: National Council of Teachers of English; Refiguring English Studies Series.

Lee, A., Williams, R., and Kilaberia, R. (2011). Engaging diversity in first-year college classrooms. *Innovative Higher Education*. doi:10.1007/s10755-011-9195-7

Lewis, M. (1992). *Shame: The exposed self*. New York: Free Press.

Light, R. J. (2001). *Making the most of college: Students speak their minds*. Cambridge, MA: Harvard University Press.

Marin, P. (2000). The educational possibility of multi-racial/multi-ethnic college classrooms. In G. Maruyama, J. F. Moreno, R. H. Gudeman, and P. Marin (Eds.), *Does diversity make a difference? Three research studies on diversity in college classrooms* (pp. 61–84). Washington, DC: American Council on Education and American Association of University Professors.

Maruyama, G., Moreno, J. F., Gudeman, R. H., and Marin, P. (2000). *Does diversity make a difference? Three research studies on diversity in college classrooms*. Washington, DC: American Council on Education and American Association of University Professors.

Mayhew, M. J., and DeLuca Fernández, S. D. (2007). Pedagogical practices that contribute to social justice outcomes. *Review of Higher Education*, *31*(1), 55–80.

Mayhew, M. J., and Grunwald, H. E. (2006). Factors contributing to faculty incorporation of diversity-related course content. *Journal of Higher Education*, *77*(1), 148–168.

McGee Banks, C. A., and Banks, J. A. (1995). Equity pedagogy: An essential component of multicultural education. *Theory Into Practice, 34*(3), 152–158. doi:10.1080/00405849509543674

McKinney, J. P., McKinney, K. G., Franiuk, R., and Schweitzer, J. (2006). The college classroom as a community: Impact on student attitudes and learning. *College Teaching, 54*(3), 281–284. doi:10.3200/CTCH.54.3.281–284

Mestenhauser, J. A. (1998). Portraits of an international curriculum: An uncommon multidimensional perspective. In J. A. Mestenhauser and B. J. Ellingboe (Eds.), *Reforming the higher education curriculum: Internationalizing the campus* (pp. 3–39). Phoenix: Oryx Press.

Milem, J. F. (2003). The educational benefits of diversity: Evidence from multiple sectors. In M. J. Chang (Ed.), *Compelling interest: Examining the evidence on racial dynamics in colleges and universities* (pp. 126–169). Stanford, CA: Stanford Education.

Milem, J. F., Chang, M. J., and Antonio, A. L. (2005). *Making diversity work on campus: A research-based perspective*. Washington, DC: Association of American Colleges and Universities.

Montoya, M. E. (2000). Silence and silencing: Their centripetal and centrifugal forces in legal communication, pedagogy and discourse. *University of Michigan Journal of Law Reform, 33*, 263–328.

Moran, R. T., Youngdahl, W. E., and Moran, S. V. (2009). Intercultural competence in business-leading global projects: Bridging the cultural and functional-divide. In D. K. Deardorff (Ed.), *The Sage Handbook of Intercultural Competence* (pp. 287–304). Thousand Oaks, CA: Sage.

Nagda, B. R., and Gurin, P. (2007). Intergroup dialogue: A critical-dialogic approach to learning about difference, inequality, and social justice. *New Directions for Teaching and Learning, 111*, 35–45.

Nelson, C. E. (1994). Critical thinking and collaborative learning. *New Directions for Teaching and Learning, 59*, 45–48. San Francisco: Jossey-Bass.

Nelson Laird, T. F., and Engberg, M. E. (2009, November). Establishing differences between diversity requirements and other courses with varying degrees of diversity inclusivity. Paper presented at the Annual Meeting of the Association for the Study of Higher Education, Vancouver, Canada.

Okayama, C. M, Furuto, S., and Edmondson J. (2001). Components of cultural competence: Attitudes, knowledge, and skills. In R. Fong and S. Furuto (Eds.), *Culturally competent practice: Skills, interventions, and evaluations* (pp. 89–100). Boston: Allyn & Bacon.

Olson, C. L., Evans, R., and Shoenberg, R. E. (2007). *At home in the world: Bridging the gap between internationalization and multicultural education*. Washington, DC: American Council on Education.

Otten, M. (2003). Intercultural learning and diversity in higher education. *Journal of Studies in International Education, 7*(1), 12.

Paige, R. M. (1993). On the nature of intercultural experiences and intercultural education. In R. M. Paige (Ed.), *Education for the intercultural experience* (2nd ed., pp. 1–19). Yarmouth, ME: Intercultural Press.

Pascarella, E., and Terenzini, P. (2005). *How college affects students: Vol. 2. A third decade of research.* San Francisco: Jossey-Bass.

Perry, W. G. (1999). *Forms of ethical and intellectual development in the college years: A scheme.* San Francisco: Jossey-Bass.

Pettigrew, T. F. (2008). Future directions for intergroup contact theory and research. *International Journal of Intercultural Relations, 32*(3), 187–199.

Pettigrew, T. F., and Tropp, L. R. (2006). A meta-analytic test of intergroup contact theory. *Journal of Personality and Social Psychology, 90*(5), 751.

Pettigrew, T. F., and Tropp, L. R. (2008). How does intergroup contact reduce prejudice? Meta-analytic tests of three mediators. *European Journal of Social Psychology, 38*(6), 922–934.

Piaget, J. (1967). *Six psychological studies.* New York: Vintage.

Pope, R., and Mueller, J. A. (2005). Faculty and curriculum: Examining multicultural competence and Inclusion. *Journal of College Student Development, 46*(6), 679–688. doi:10.1353/csd.2005.0065

Pope, R. L., and Reynolds, A. L. (1997). Student affairs core competencies: Integrating multicultural awareness, knowledge, and skills. *Journal of College Student Development, 38,* 266–277.

Pusch, M. D. (2009). The interculturally competent global leader. In D. K. Deardorff (Ed.), *The Sage handbook of intercultural competence* (pp. 66–84). Thousand Oaks, CA: Sage.

Quaye, S. J., and Harper, S. R. (2009). *Student engagement in higher education: Theoretical perspectives and practical approaches for diverse populations.* New York: Taylor & Francis.

Rathje, S. (2007). Intercultural competence: The status and future of a controversial concept. *Language and Intercultural Communication, 7*(4), 254–266.

Regents of the University of California v. Bakke, 438 U.S. 265 (1978).

Rendón, L. I. (1994). Validating culturally diverse students: Towards a new model of learning and student development. *Innovative Higher Education, 19*(1), 33–50.

Rendón, L. I. (2005). Realizing a transformed pedagogical dreamfield: Recasting agreements for teaching and learning. *Spirituality in Higher Education Newsletter.*

Richards, S. L. F. (2003). The interactive syllabus: A resource-based, constructivist approach to learning. *The Technology Source.* Available at http://www.technologysource.org /article/interactive syllabus/

Roark, J. L., and others. (2011). *Understanding the American promise: A brief history.* Boston: Bedford St. Martin's.

Rothwell, A. (2005). Think global, teach local. *Innovations in Education and Teaching International, 42*(4), 313–323. doi:10.1080/14703290500291875

Rypisi, C., Malcolm, L. E., and Kim, H. S. (2009). Environmental and developmental approach to supporting women's success in STEM fields. In S. R. Harper and S. J. Quaye (Eds.), *Student engagement in higher education: Theoretical perspectives and practical approaches for diverse populations* (pp. 1–12). New York: Routledge.

Saenz, V. B. (2010). Breaking the segregation cycle: Examining students' precollege racial environments and college diversity experiences. *Review of Higher Education, 34*(1), 1–37.

Saenz, V. B., Ngai, H. N., and Hurtado, S. (2007). Factors influencing positive interactions across race for African American, Asian American, Latino, and White college students. *Research in Higher Education, 48*(1), 1–38.

Sampson, J., and Cohen, R. (2001). Design peer learning. In D. Boud, R. Cohen, and J. Sampson (Eds.), *Peer learning in higher education* (pp. 35–49). London: Kogan Page.

Sargent, S. E., Sedlak, C. A., and Martsolf, D. S. (2005). Cultural competence among nursing students and faculty. *Nursing Education Today, 25*(3), 214–221.

Schuerholz-Lehr, S. (2007). Teaching for global literacy in higher education: How prepared are the educators? *Journal of Studies in International Education, 11*(2), 180.

Sheets, R. H. (2005). *Diversity pedagogy: Examining the role of culture in the teaching-learning process.* Boston: Allyn & Bacon.

Sheets, R. H. (2009). What is diversity pedagogy? *Multicultural Education, 16*(3), 11.

Simon, R. (1988). Empowerment as a pedagogy of possibility. *Language Arts, 64,* 370–382.

Slavin, R. E. (1995). *Cooperative learning: Theory, research, and practice* (2nd ed.). Boston: Allyn & Bacon.

Smith, D. G. (2010). *Diversity's promise for higher education.* Baltimore: Johns Hopkins University Press.

Spitzberg, B. H. (2003). Methods of skill assessment. In J. O. Greene and B. R. Burleson (Eds.), *Handbook of communication and social interaction skills.* Mahwah, NJ: Erlbaum.

Spitzberg, B. H., and Changnon, G. (2009). Conceptualizing intercultural competence. In D. K. Deardorff (Ed.), *The Sage handbook of intercultural competence* (pp. 2–52). Thousand Oaks, CA: Sage.

Spitzberg, B. H., and Cupach, W. R. (1989). *Handbook of interpersonal competence research.* New York: Springer-Verlag.

Steele, C. M. (1997). A threat in the air: How stereotypes shape intellectual identity and performance. *American Psychologist, 52*(6), 613.

Stenberg, S., and Lee, A. (2002). Developing pedagogies: Learning the teaching of English. *College English, 64*(3), 326–347.

Stephan, W. G., and Stephan, C. W. (1985). Intergroup anxiety. *Journal of Social Issues, 41*(3), 157–175.

Stewart, D. L. (2008). Confronting the politics of multicultural competence. *About Campus, 13*(1), 10–17.

Tatum, B. D. (1992). Talking about race, learning about racism: The application of racial identity development theory in the classroom. *Harvard Educational Review, 62*(1), 1–25.

Ting-Toomey, S. (2005). Identity negotiation theory: Crossing cultural boundaries. In W. B. Gudykunst (Ed.), *Theorizing about intercultural communication* (pp. 211–233). Thousand Oaks, CA: Sage.

Ting-Toomey, S., and Kurogi, A. (1998). Facework competence in intercultural conflict: An updated face-negotiation theory. *International Journal of Intercultural Relations, 22,* 187–225.

Trimble, J. E., Pedersen, P. B., and Rodela, E. S. (2009). The real cost of intercultural incompetence: An epilogue. In D. K Deardorff (Ed.), *The Sage handbook of intercultural competence* (pp. 492–503). Thousand Oaks, CA: Sage.

Turner, J. E., and Schallert, D. L. (2001). Expectancy–value relationships of shame reactions and shame resiliency. *Journal of Educational Psychology, 93*(2), 320–329. doi:10.1037/0022-0663.93.2.320

Turniansky, B., and others. (2009). From the inside out: Learning to understand and appreciate multiple voices through telling identities. *New Directions for Teaching and Learning, 118*, 39–47. doi:10.1002/tl

Twenge, J. M., and others. (2008). Egos inflating over time: A cross-temporal meta-analysis of the narcissistic personality inventory. *Journal of Personality, 76*(4), 875–902.

Umbach, P. D., and Wawrzynski, M. R. (2005). Faculty do matter: The role of college faculty in student learning and engagement. *Research in Higher Education, 46*(2), 153–184.

Van de Vijver, J. R., and Leung, K. (2009) Methodological issues in researching intercultural competence. In D. K. Deardorff (Ed.), *The Sage handbook of intercultural competence* (pp. 404–418). Thousand Oaks, CA: Sage.

VanDeWeghe, R., and Reid, L. (2000). Reading the classroom as text: A heuristic for classroom inquiry. *English Education, 32*(2), 127–140.

Van Ek, J. A. (1986). *Objectives for foreign language teaching* (Vol.1). Croton, NY: Manhattan.

Van Gyn, G., Schuerholz-Lehr, S., Caws, C., and Preece, A. (2009). Education for world-mindedness: Beyond superficial notions of internationalization. *New Directions for Teaching and Learning, 118*, 25–38.

Webb, N. M., Ender, P., and Lewis, S. (1986). Problem-solving strategies and group processes in small groups learning computer programming. *American Educational Research Journal, 23*(2), 243–261.

Weinstein, G., and Obear, K. (1992). Bias issues in the classroom: Encounters with the teaching self. *New Directions for Teaching and Learning, 52*, 39–50.

Wenger, E., and Snyder, W. M. (2000, January–February). Communities of practice: The organizational frontier. *Harvard Business Review,* pp. 139–145.

Wildman, S. M. (1995). Privilege and liberalism in legal education: Teaching and learning in a diverse environment. *Berkeley Women's Law Journal, 10*, 88–98.

Williams, D. A., Berger, J. B., and McClendon, S. (2005). *Toward a model of inclusive excellence and change in postsecondary institutions.* Washington, DC: Association of American Colleges and Universities.

Wong, M. S. (2006). *Supporting diversity and internationalization through transformative learning experiences.* Urbana, IL: Forum on Public Policy.

Yershova, Y., DeJeaghere, J., and Mestenhauser, J. (2000). Thinking not as usual: Adding the intercultural perspective. *Journal of Studies in International Education, 4*(1), 59–78.

Name Index

A

Adler, P. S., 25
Alger, J. R., 5
Allport, W., 3, 4, 70, 80
Anderson, J., 68
Antonio, A. L., 1, 3, 6, 8, 15, 16–17, 19, 71
Arasaratnam, L. A., 30, 37
Arkoudis, S., 3
Association of American Colleges and Universities, 3

B

Banks, J., 47
Banks, J. A., 15, 47
Barker, S., 100
Batson, C. D., 25
Baxter Magolda, M. B., 25, 26, 33, 95
Bennett, D. L., 27
Bennett, J. M., 27, 30
Bennett J. M., 38
Bennett, M. J., 25
Berger, J. B., 5, 6, 16
Bok, D., 50
Boler, M., 57
Bowman, N. A., 3
Bridges, B. K., 7
Brown-Jeffy, S., 81
Bruffee, K. A., 55
Buckley, J. A., 7

Bushman, B. J., 31
Byram, M., 25

C

Caws, C., 48, 89
Chang, J. C., 12
Chang, M. J., 3, 4, 5, 6, 12, 55
Changnon, G., 25
Chávez, A. F., 47
Christensen, L., 61
Clayton-Pedersen, A. R., 6
Clifford, J., 61
Cohen, P. C., 68
Cohen, R., 70
Cook, J., 25
Cooper, J. E., 81
Crichton, J., 100
Cupach, W., 25
Cupach, W. R., 26
Curtis, M., 13

D

Danowitz, M. A., 11, 49, 56, 66, 67
Day, P., 52
Deardorff, D. K., 2
Dehert, K., 73
DeJeaghere, J., 3, 95
DeLuca Fernández, S. D., 14
Denson, N., 3, 4, 5, 19, 55
Dewey, J., 11

Dey, E. L., 3, 4, 5, 7, 16, 20, 60, 80
Dobbert, M., 47
Doerfel, M. L., 30, 37

E
Edmondson J., 25, 30
Eisenchlas, S., 11
Ellsworth, E., 61
Ender, P., 71
Engberg, M. E., 68, 79
Equality Challenge Unit, 18
Evans, R., 12, 15, 18, 52

F
Foster, J. D., 31
Franiuk, R., 99
Furuto, S., 25, 30

G
Gair, M., 60
Gallagher, C., 37
Gay, G., 16
Gesche, A., 5, 28, 82
Glenn, W., 11
Goldberg, C., 97
Gonzales, M. H., 86
Goodman, C. C., 86
Goodman, D. J., 56
Gore, J., 61
Gottfredson, N. C., 3
Grandin, J. M., 3
Green, M. F., 15
Grunwald, H. E., 9
Gudeman, R. H., 9
Gudykunst, W. B., 14
Guido-DiBrito, F., 65
Gurin, G., 3, 4, 5, 7, 60, 80
Gurin, P., 3, 4, 5, 7, 16, 58, 60, 80

H
Hanson, L., 48, 89
Harper, S. R., 1, 7, 11, 52, 56
Hartley, C. C., 59
Hartman, S. M., 68
Haskins, C. H., 103

Hayek, J. C., 7
Hedderich, N., 3
Herrington, A., 13
Hoffman, D. M., 18
Hoskins, J., 75
Howard-Hamilton, M., 23
Hsing, C., 33, 40
Hu, S., 3, 4
Hunter, W., 25
Hurtado, S., 3, 4, 5, 7, 8, 11, 19, 55, 58, 60, 70, 71, 80, 84, 89, 91, 92, 93

I
Ickes, W., 84
Imahori, T. T., 25
Inoue, Y., 9, 47

J
Johnson, D. W., 71
Johnson, K., 9, 47
Johnson, M. P., 68
Johnson, R. T., 71

K
Kegan, R., 25
Keith Campbell, W., 31
Kezar, A., 11
Khaja, K., 9
Kilaberia, R., 53, 75, 95
Kim, H. S., 62
Kim, Y. Y., 26
King, A., 70
King, P., 23
King, P. M., 25, 26, 33, 95
Kinzie, J., 7
Kolb, D. A., 53
Konrath, S., 31
Konrath, S. H., 33, 40
Krutky, J., 5, 45, 46, 48
Kuh, G. D., 3, 4, 7
Kumagai, A. K., 3, 15, 45, 52, 57, 58, 65, 78, 99
Kurogi, A., 38
Kuszewski, A., 54

L

Ladson-Billings, G., 15
Lagos, A., 73
Langer, E. J., 27
Lawson, A., 68
Ledesma, M. C., 12
Lee, A., 37, 50, 53, 60, 75, 76, 95
Lester, J., 11
Leung, K., 29
Lewis, M., 97
Lewis, S., 71
Light, R. J., 60
Lishner, D. A., 25
Lopez, G. E., 70
Lypson, M. L., 3, 15, 45, 52, 57, 58, 65, 78, 99

M

Makeham, P., 5, 28, 82
Malcolm, L. E., 62
Mallory, S. L., 65
Marin, P., 5, 9
Martsolf, D. S., 3
Maruyama, G., 9
Mayhew, M. J., 9, 14
McClendon, S., 5, 6, 16
McGee Banks, C. A., 47
McGee, C. A., 15
McKinney, J. P., 99
McKinney, K. G., 99
Mestenhauser, J., 3, 15, 25, 95
Mestenhauser, J. A., 11, 47
Milem, J. F., 3
Moldoveanu, M., 48
Montoya, M. E., 100
Moran, R. T., 3
Moran, S. V., 3
Moreno, J. F., 9
Mueller, J. A., 9
Mullins, G., 60
Musil, C. M., 6

N

Nagda, B. R., 58
Nagda, B. R. A., 16, 20, 70

Nakamoto, J., 11
Nelson, C. E., 55
Nelson Laird, T. F., 68, 79
Ngai, H. N., 3

O

Obear, K., 85, 87–88, 89, 90
O'Brien, E. H., 33, 40
Okayama, C. M, 25, 30
Olson, C. L., 12, 15, 18, 52
O'Neill, N., 6
Otten, M., 5, 15, 18, 29, 46, 47, 70

P

Paige, R. M., 38
Pascarella, E., 2
Pedersen, P. B., 38
Perry, W. G., 33
Petrucci, C. J., 59
Pettigrew, T. F., 3
Piaget, J., 55
Poch, R., 73, 75
Pope, R., 9
Pope, R. L., 26, 29, 38
Preece, A., 48, 89
Pusch, M. D., 27

Q

Quaye, S. J., 7, 52, 56

R

Rathje, S., 26
Reid, L., 61
Rendón, L. I., 10
Reynolds, A. L., 26, 29, 38
Richards, S. L. F., 68
Roark, J. L., 68
Rodela, E. S., 38
Rothwell, A., 9
Rypisi, C., 62

S

Saenz, V. B., 2
Salonen, R., 30, 38, 48
Sampson, J., 70

Sargent, S. E., 3
Sawyer, S., 25
Schallert, D. L., 97
Schuerholz-Lehr, S., 9
Schweitzer, J., 99
Sedlak, C. A., 3
Shapiro, R., 84
Sheets, R. H., 66
Shoenberg, R., 15
Shoenberg, R. E., 12, 15, 18, 52
Simon, R., 50
Slavin, R. E., 93
Smith, D. G., 4
Smith, K. A., 71
Snyder, W. M., 70
Spitzberg, B. H., 25, 26
Stage, S., 68
Steele, C. M., 62
Stenberg, S., 60
Stephan, C. W., 40
Stephan, W. G., 40
Stewart, D. L., 61

T
Tatum, B. D., 62
Terenzini, P., 2
Ting-Toomey, S., 10, 25, 33, 38, 40, 86
Trevaskes, S., 11
Trimble, J. E., 38

Tropp, L. R., 3, 59, 89
Tuitt, F., 11, 49, 56, 66, 67
Turner, J. E., 97
Turniansky, B., 75
Twenge, J. M., 31

U
Umbach, P. D., 31

V
Van de Vijver, J. R., 29
Van Ek, J. A., 37
Van Gyn, 48, 89
VanDeWeghe, R., 61

W
Wawrzynski, M. R., 7
Webb, N. M., 71
Weinstein, G., 85, 87–88, 89, 90
Wenger, E., 70
Wildman, S. M., 61
Williams, D. A., 5, 6, 16
Williams, R., 53, 75, 95
Wong, M. S., 5, 18, 55, 92, 93

Y
Yershova, Y., 3, 25, 95
Youngdahl, W. E., 3

Subject Index

A

Abstract conceptualization, 53
Academic skill development, 3
Academic writing, 13
Achievement barrier, negative stereotypes as, 62
Active experimentation, 53
Affective domain in the classroom, acknowledging, 89
Ambiguity, model tolerance for, 87–89
Anxiety: acknowledging, 84–89; addressing directly, 88; excessive, 86; managing, 40–42; support, offering, 85–86; thresholds of, 85–86

B

Balance: between constructive critique and suspending judgment, 94–95; of support and dissonance, 57–59
Behavioral changes toward others, 27
Biased comments, responding to, 89–90
Biographical information, incorporating into a class, 77

C

Classroom: as privileged space, 60–63; social relations in, 89–93
Cognitive sophistication/complexity, 3
Collaborative learning: and self-grouping, 91; techniques, 53–54

Collaborative tasks, assigning, 92–94
Collective agreements about behaviors/values in learning environment, 81
College classrooms: opportunities for student contributions, 83–84; practices essential in context of, 67
Communication, welcoming different styles of, 99–100
Composition studies, 13
Comprehension, 34–35
Concrete experience, 53
Conditional language, 68–69
Content-based pedagogy, 47–49, 52
Course design: aligning multiple dimensions to reflect importance of engaging diversity, 67; biographical information, incorporating into a class, 77; collaborative learning, 71–72; communication and collaboration, 72; conditional language, 68–69; engaging diversity, establishing an environment supporting, 80–82; experiential knowledge, incorporating opportunities to apply, 74–78; explicit identification of relevant intercultural skills, behaviors, and attitudes, 78–80; incorporating intercultural pedagogical principles into, 66–82; intercultural encounters facilitating effects opposed to desired outcomes, 70; literature providing

instructor guidance related to cooperative/collaborative learning, 70; narrative inquiry, 74–75; positive outcomes among participants of equal status, 80–81; reflection of application of experiential knowledge, 77; reflection of student's exposure to classmates' experiential knowledge, 78; reflection/perspective taking, providing opportunities for, 68–69; respectful classroom environment, building, 80; structuring collaboration/interaction opportunities with diverse peers, 70–74; value of interactions, allocating time to signal, 72–73

Critical engagement, distinguishing from premature judgment, 32

Critical pedagogies, 17–18, 81

Critical thinking skills, 3

Critique, and shame, 97–98

Cultural artifacts, course involving the sharing of, 75

Cultural awareness, 34–36

Cultural stereotypes, 62–63

Culturally relevant pedagogy, 81

Curiosity/discovery, 29, 33–34

D

Demographics, presence of difference in, 7

Disciplinary knowledge, and learning how to teach, 51

Dissonance, 89

Diverse classrooms, promise/challenge of, 8–9

Diversity, *See also* Engaging diversity: building into the center of higher education, 12; defined, 6, 6–7; in early college years, 8; effectively engaging, 2; employer-based rationale for, 3–4; engaging for intercultural outcomes, 4–7; factoring into the creation of student groups, 9; happy, 94; inclusive excellence, 6; integrating, 12–13; and multicultural course content, 4; "performance" of a positive attitude

toward, 94–95; piecemeal approach to, 11; as reflection of, 2; structural, 5; and student outcomes, 10; students as reflection of, 2

Diversity requirement, 11; incorporating, 11–12

E

Employers, and intercultural skills, 3–4

Engagement, 7

Engaging diversity, 6–9; in the classroom, 6, 8, 16, 82; and conceptualization of instruction, 49; contribution to growth of higher-order cognitive skills, 3; core premise of, 66; and culturally inclusive pedagogical approaches/resources, 16–17; facilitating purposeful interactions, 70; and fostering intercultural interactions in the classroom, 50, 52; pedagogy, practicing, 83–101; and student view of peers, 89; theoretical framework for, 65–66; through course design and preparation, 65–82

Equity pedagogy, 81

Experiential knowledge, incorporating opportunities to apply, 74–78

F

Faculty development: lessons on, 14–15; models, 60

Feedback: on development of intercultural competence, 70; written, on small-group work, 92

Fisher v. University of Texas at Austin, 105

G

Gratz v. Bollinger, 106

Group differences, 7

Grutter v. Bollinger, 106

H

Happy diversity, 94

Holistic approach, 25

I

Inclusive dialogue, 98–100
Inclusive engagement of diversity in higher education, 10
Inclusive excellence, foundational premise of, 6
Individual differences, 7
Integrated approach, achieving, 13–14
Integration, need for, 17–18
Interaction, managing the stages of, 98–99
Intercultural competence, 1–21, 29; anxiety, managing, 40–42; building blocks of, 26–27; component-based models, 29; comprehension, 34–35; core premises of, 24–26; cultural awareness, 34–36; cultural self-awareness, development of, 42; curiosity/discovery, 29, 33–34; Deardorff's model of, 27; developing a pedagogy supporting, 45–63; developmental outcomes, 39–43; foundational knowledge, importance of, 23–24; intercultural skills, 34, 38–39; knowledge, 27, 34–35; motivation, 27; new categories for diverse strangers, 40; openness, 29, 32–33; pedagogical capacity to support, 46; as priority and educational outcomes of higher education, 2–3; process model, 28; process of, 27–39; respect, 29, 30–32; self-awareness, 34–35; skills, 27; sociolinguistic awareness, 36–38; uncertainty, managing, 40–42; understanding, 23–43
Intercultural competency skills, development of, 8–9
Intercultural development process, 27–29
Intercultural learning: integrated framework for, 53–54; and pendulum of external/internal reflection, 69–70
Intercultural mind-set, 27
Intercultural pedagogical principles, 55–59, 65–66; anxiety, acknowledging, 84–89; applying to classroom facilitation, 84–100; balance of support and dissonance, 57–59; incorporating into

course design, 66–82; maximization/facilitation of purposeful interactions, 55–56; valuing assets students bring to classroom, 56–57
Intercultural pedagogy, 49–52; classrooms as privileged spaces, 60–63; developing, 50–51, 59–60; and effects of instruction, acknowledgement of, 52; foundational principles, 55–59, 65–66; pedagogical actions, 65
Intercultural skills, 8, 34, 38–39; call for, 2–4; and employers, 3–4; undergraduate education to support development of, 3
Intergroup contact, in diversity-related learning and development outcomes, 4
Internationalization of the curriculum, 48
Invisible differences, 7
Islands of innovation, 11

J

Journals, 19, 50, 75, 77, 81, 86
Judgment, suspending, 32, 39, 94–95, 97

K

Knowledge, 34–35; experiential, incorporating opportunities to apply, 74–78; foundational, importance of, 23–24; and intercultural competence, 27, 34–35

L

Language, conditional, 68–69
Leadership skills, development of, 3
Learning: collaborative, 53–54, 91; intercultural, 53–54, 69–70; process, stages of, 53

M

Magical thinking, and diversity, 12
Mindfulness, need for, 52
Mindlessness, 10, 52
Multicultural contexts, teaching/learning in, 91
Multicultural education theory, essential dimension, 48

N

Narrative inquiry, 74–75
Negative stereotypes, 62

O

Openness, 29, 32–33

P

Pedagogical resources, and empowerment of students, 16–17
Pedagogical training, 20
Pedagogy: and connections between who/what/how of teaching and learning, 50; critical, 17–18, 81; developing to support intercultural competence, 45–63; engaging diversity, 83–101; in higher education, content-focused model of, 47–49, 52; institutional context, 46–47; intercultural, 49–52
Peer review, 95–96
Personal and Social Responsibility Inventory (PSRI), 4
Power, and social identities, 48
Prejudice, reducing, 3
Privilege, and social identities, 48
Privileged space, classroom as, 60–63
Purposeful small groups, facilitation of, 91–92

R

Racial/cultural appreciation, increasing, 3
Reflective learning journals, 19, 50, 75, 77, 81, 86
Reflective observation, 53
Reflective writing, on formative experience in educational settings, 81–82
Regents of the University of California v. Bakke, 106
Respect, 29, 30–32
Respectful classroom environment, building, 80

S

Self-awareness, 34–35
Self-grouping: and collaborative learning, 91; habits, challenging, 90–91
Shame, and critique, 97–98
Social constructions of identity, 62
Social differences, 7
Social justice-oriented learning outcomes, practices contributing to, 67
Social relations in the classroom: biased comments, responding to, 89–90; collaborative tasks, assigning, 92–94; disrupting, 89–93; purposeful small groups, facilitation of, 91–92; self-grouping habits, challenging, 90–91; triggers, responding to, 89–90
Sociolinguistic awareness, 36–38
Staggered small-group experience, 92
Stereotypes, cultural, 62–63
Structural diversity, 5
Student contributions, opportunities for, 83–84
Student perspectives, 19
Student self-identity, affirming, 86–87
Student voices, reflections on engaging diversity, 18–19
Student writing, feedback on development of intercultural competence, 70
Students: common aspirations, 2; as reflection of diversity, 2
Suspending judgment, 32, 39; and constructive critique, balance between, 94–95; and developing critical thinking skills, modeling the balance of, 97; as prerequisite for critical thinking, 95

T

Tasks, collaborative, 92–94
Teaching in multicultural contexts, 91
Tensions, and development of intercultural competency, 15

Thresholds of anxiety, 85–86
Training, pedagogical, 20
Transformative/integrated approach: lack
   of, 15; need for, 12–13
Triggers, responding to, 89–90

U

Underground (short film), 73
Understanding the American Promise (Roark
   and others), 68–69

V

Validating critique, 97–98
Voice, and social identities, 48

W

Writing: academic, 13; reflective, 81–82;
   student, and feedback on development
   of intercultural competence, 70
Written communication, and development
   of intercultural competency, 13–14
Written feedback, on small-group work, 92

About the Authors

Amy Lee is a faculty member in the Department of Postsecondary Teaching and Learning at the University of Minnesota. She has published on critical pedagogy and writing studies, including *Teaching Writing That Matters* with Chris Gallagher (2008) and *Composing Critical Pedagogies* (2001). Amy's recent research is on pedagogy that supports critical intercultural competency and inclusive excellence. She has taught writing, literature, and theory courses to diverse populations of students, from the first-year to the doctoral level. Amy has served in administrative positions at various public research universities: department chair, director of undergraduate writing studies major, and writing program director. She received a University of Minnesota Distinguished Teaching Award, and a University of Massachusetts–Amherst University Distinguished Teaching Award.

Robert Poch is a Senior Fellow in the Department of Postsecondary Teaching and Learning at the University of Minnesota. His publications include an ASHE-ERIC monograph, *Academic Freedom in American Higher Education*, as well as research on state and federal higher education policy. Currently, Robert is researching the pedagogy and course content used in law schools to prepare civil rights attorneys prior to the 1954 *Brown v. Board of Education* decision. Robert teaches undergraduate history courses and a graduate course on multicultural theories of college student development applied to teaching and learning. He is the former state higher education executive officer for Minnesota.

Amy Lee is lead author: all authors are listed alphabetically.

Marta Shaw is a PhD candidate in comparative and international development education in the Department of Organizational Leadership, Policy, and Development at the University of Minnesota. Her research is focused on the impact of globalization on higher education governance, research integrity, and intercultural education. Her recent research has examined intercultural competence development at the undergraduate level in the United States, higher education reform in Poland, the impact of the Bologna Process on academic staff in Ukraine, and integrity in international research collaborations.

Rhiannon D. Williams is currently the Director of Assessment for the First-Year Experience program in the Department of Postsecondary Teaching and Learning at the University of Minnesota. Rhiannon has been involved in several research projects related to the monograph: Study Abroad Curriculum Integration, Learning Communities, and assessment of the First-Year Experience program in the College of Education and Human Development. In the spring of 2010, she completed and defended her dissertation, titled *Constructions of Equitable Notions of Quality in Early Childhood Care and Development from Two Communities in the Philippines: Local Practices of Bayanihan and Dagyaw.*

About the ASHE Higher Education Report Series

Since 1983, the ASHE (formerly ASHE-ERIC) Higher Education Report Series has been providing researchers, scholars, and practitioners with timely and substantive information on the critical issues facing higher education. Each monograph presents a definitive analysis of a higher education problem or issue, based on a thorough synthesis of significant literature and institutional experiences. Topics range from planning to diversity and multiculturalism, to performance indicators, to curricular innovations. The mission of the Series is to link the best of higher education research and practice to inform decision making and policy. The reports connect conventional wisdom with research and are designed to help busy individuals keep up with the higher education literature. Authors are scholars and practitioners in the academic community. Each report includes an executive summary, review of the pertinent literature, descriptions of effective educational practices, and a summary of key issues to keep in mind to improve educational policies and practice.

The Series is one of the most peer reviewed in higher education. A National Advisory Board made up of ASHE members reviews proposals. A National Review Board of ASHE scholars and practitioners reviews completed manuscripts. Six monographs are published each year and they are approximately 144 pages in length. The reports are widely disseminated through Jossey-Bass and John Wiley & Sons, and they are available online to subscribing institutions through Wiley Online Library (http://wileyonlinelibrary.com).

Call for Proposals

The ASHE Higher Education Report Series is actively looking for proposals. We encourage you to contact one of the editors, Dr. Kelly Ward (kaward@wsu.edu) or Dr. Lisa Wolf-Wendel (lwolf@ku.edu), with your ideas.

Recent Titles

Volume 38 ASHE Higher Education Report

1. Creating a Tipping Point: Strategic Human Resources in Higher Education
    Alvin Evans and Edna Chun

Volume 37 ASHE Higher Education Report

1. Women's Status in Higher Education: Equity Matters
    Elizabeth J. Allan

2. Philanthropy and Fundraising in American Higher Education
    Noah D. Drezner

3. Veterans in Higher Education: When Johnny and Jane Come Marching to Campus
    David DiRamio and Kathryn Jarvis

4. Stonewall's Legacy: Bisexual, Gay, Lesbian, and Transgender Students in Higher Education
    Susan B. Marine

5. Postsecondary Education for American Indian and Alaska Natives: Higher Education
    for Nation Building and Self-Determination
    *Bryan McKinley Jones Brayboy, Amy J. Fann, Angelina E. Castagno, and
    Jessica A. Solyom*

6. Qualitative Inquiry for Equity in Higher Education: Methodological Innovations, Impli-
    cations, and Interventions
    Penny A. Pasque, Rozana Carducci, Aaron M. Kuntz, and Ryan Evely Gildersleeve

Volume 36 ASHE Higher Education Report

1. Cultural Capital: The Promises and Pitfalls in Educational Research
    Rachelle Winkle-Wagner

2. Partnerships and Collaborations in Higher Education
    Pamela L. Eddy

3. The Global Growth of Private Higher Education
    *Kevin Kinser, Daniel C. Levy, Juan Carlos Silas Casillas, Andrés Bernasconi, Snejana
    Slantcheva-Durst, Wycliffe Otieno, Jason E. Lane, Prachayani Praphamontripong,
    William Zumeta, and Robin LaSota*

4. Understanding the New Majority of Non-Tenure-Track Faculty in Higher Education:
    Demographics, Experiences, and Plans of Action
    Adrianna Kezar and Cecile Sam

5. Non-Tenure-Track Faculty in Higher Education: Theories and Tensions
    Adrianna Kezar and Cecile Sam

6. Racial and Ethnic Minority Students' Success in STEM Education
    Samuel D. Museus, Robert T. Palmer, Ryan J. Davis, and Dina C. Maramba

Volume 35 ASHE Higher Education Report

1. Bridging the Diversity Divide: Globalization and Reciprocal Empowerment in Higher Education
    Edna Chun and Alvin Evans

2. Understanding Interdisciplinary Challenges and Opportunities in Higher Education
    Karri A. Holley

3. Ethnic and Racial Administrative Diversity: Understanding Work Life Realities and Experiences
    in Higher Education

ORDER FORM SUBSCRIPTION AND SINGLE ISSUES

DISCOUNTED BACK ISSUES:

Use this form to receive 20% off all back issues of *ASHE Higher Education Report.*
All single issues priced at **$23.20** (normally $29.00)

TITLE	ISSUE NO.	ISBN
_____	_____	_____
_____	_____	_____
_____	_____	_____

Call 888-378-2537 or see mailing instructions below. When calling, mention the promotional code JBNND to receive your discount. For a complete list of issues, please visit www.josseybass.com/go/aehe

SUBSCRIPTIONS: (1 YEAR, 6 ISSUES)

☐ New Order   ☐ Renewal

U.S.	☐ Individual: $174	☐ Institutional: $281
CANADA/MEXICO	☐ Individual: $174	☐ Institutional: $341
ALL OTHERS	☐ Individual: $210	☐ Institutional: $392

Call 888-378-2537 or see mailing and pricing instructions below.
Online subscriptions are available at www.onlinelibrary.wiley.com

ORDER TOTALS:

Issue / Subscription Amount: $ _____

Shipping Amount: $ _____
(for single issues only – subscription prices include shipping)

Total Amount: $ _____

SHIPPING CHARGES:	
First Item	$6.00
Each Add'l Item	$2.00

(No sales tax for U.S. subscriptions. Canadian residents, add GST for subscription orders. Individual rate subscriptions must be paid by personal check or credit card. Individual rate subscriptions may not be resold as library copies.)

BILLING & SHIPPING INFORMATION:

☐ **PAYMENT ENCLOSED:** *(U.S. check or money order only. All payments must be in U.S. dollars.)*

☐ **CREDIT CARD:**   ☐ VISA   ☐ MC   ☐ AMEX

Card number _____ Exp. Date_____

Card Holder Name_____ Card Issue # _____

Signature _____ Day Phone_____

☐ **BILL ME:** *(U.S. institutional orders only. Purchase order required.)*

Purchase order # _____
Federal Tax ID 13559302 • GST 89102-8052

Name _____

Address_____

Phone_____ E-mail_____

Copy or detach page and send to: **John Wiley & Sons, One Montgomery Street, Suite 1200, San Francisco, CA 94104-4594**

Order Form can also be faxed to: **888-481-2665**

PROMO JBNND